Behind the
BLACK
MIRROR

BLANCHE PARKER

ISBN 978-1-0980-9414-0 (paperback)
ISBN 978-1-0980-9415-7 (digital)

Christian Faith Publishing, Inc.
832 Park Avenue
Meadville, PA 16335
www.christianfaithpublishing.com

Printed in the United States of America

To my great-grandchildren,

Marlon
Quante
Mason
Jailynne
Amaru
Vivian
Dani
Amelia
Nyia

With hope for a better world for them and all future generations.

To my family - my granddaughter Morgan Parker and my great-grandson Amarú Parker, even across the miles, they each and every day say something for inspiration, send ideas, a new word, or listen to a sentence to hear if it sounds right or it makes sense.

I can't forget my niece, Helen Johnson, who praises me for my academic achievements, even when I was attempting to achieve a doctorate degree but didn't quite make it. She yet has praise for my book writing, really, I thought I heard her call me "Aunt Author."

Indeed, I have nothing but praise for my publishing team who dedicated their efforts and expertise from the beginning to the end in making my book a success.

Be Still, sad heart, and cease repining; Behind
the dark clouds is the sun still shining.
—Henry Wadsworth Longfellow

Be still sad America and cease repining;
Behind the Black mirror there is still a shining
light of hope in the America's promise.
—Henry Wadsworth Longfellow

We Declare these truths to be self evident
that all men are created equal, that they
are endowed by their creator with certain
unalienable Rights, that among these are
Life, Liberty and the Pursuit of Happiness.
—Henry Wadsworth Longfellow

ACKNOWLEDGEMENTS

First and foremost, I would like to express my special thanks of gratitude to my former granddaughter-in-law, Yeimy Gates, for helping pioneer this awesome journey with her expertise in technology and organization of information that is required to get started was phenomenal.

I also would like to thank her son Lucas, who was four years old at the time. Lucas is special to me as well. I wanted so much to add his name to the list of great grandsons. He calls me Grandma Park and shows so much love for me. Chris, Yeimy's husband, I would like to thank as well.

Yeimy is also an immigrant to this country who has contributed much through her academic achievements. Thank you Yeimy.

PROLOGUE

Utopia was a strange-sounding word to me seventy-seven years ago when my English teacher assigned me to deliver the end-of-year speech titled "America, the Utopia of the World." It was I—a fourteen-year-old Black girl born and reared in a small town down south where there was no school building for my first years. We attended school in private homes and the church. Later, a school building was built; it was nothing extreme, just a building resembling an elongated "H" and yellow in color.

There were only nine grades. After ninth grade, you would go to some other town to finish high school. When I was selected to deliver this speech, I was not introduced as valedictorian or the salutatorian, but I was to deliver the end-of-year speech leaving a message to those coming behind.

I have never forgotten that experience. I was asked to do the speech at my church. My mother was very proud of me.

Today, at the age of ninety-two, I have been in deep thought about why this speech has come back to me. I'm not one to believe in ghosts of the past.

One would wonder, *Why did this teacher in a small town, in a small school teaching children who have not been fifty miles away from home have faith in her students and her teachings?* But she did. Now I'm wondering why I'm so determined to delve into this topic. Is this my way of keeping that teacher's legacy alive?

A map of the world that does not include Utopia is not worth even glancing at, for it leaves out the one Country at which Humanity is always landing. And when Humanity lands there, it looks out, and, seeing a better country, sets sail. Progress is the realization of Utopias. (Oscar Wilde, *The Soul of Man Under Socialism*)

For other nations, Utopia is a blessed past never to be recovered, for Americans it is just beyond the horizon. (Henry Kissinger)

WHY I ARGUE

This book is an argument—arguing for a better world and creating a better world. The problem of creating a better world has been studied by scholars of philosophy, psychology, ethics and by spiritual groups throughout history; their interests were in solving the problems involved and the ethical dilemma for those who are founders of the idea through utopian thinking—the idea which began during the early colonial times and was acceptable by the pilgrims.

Utopia, like the Ariadne's thread, takes us through an exhaustive maze to argue Utopia. A time line stretched from the fifteenth century to our present time and with Thomas More as "Theseus" unraveling the ball of thread and illustrates the problems of the people in a capitalist and socialist society.

Capitalist was dominant of the two factions and decides the fate of the people. Fate, I mean, how will the people fare better in a capitalist society—an ideology; individuals are responsible for themselves and the society whose ideology was in the distribution of wealth with these two differing perceptions. Where does the interest lie? With God's authority, the whole world would become Utopian.

As the centuries pass and the generations change in ideologies, people's thinking changes. Some doubt that Utopia can be materialized or realized. They give reasons that people are mostly locked into their own mental institution (mindset), and in order to achieve a perfect society, the people have to be perfect; we know neither of those will happen, but the need to keep striving for a better world is worth it for all people, especially for our children.

In the Beginning

Utopia in America dates back from the 1600s at the time of the Puritan settlements who came together with other communes with shared visions. It was clear in the heart of the wilderness to carve a community so that they could create a society of social and civil disobedience. It was accepted by the European communities. There were some differences, however; they espoused the pursuit of happiness as an "unalienable right." Albeit, their inspirations varied as it relates to their philosophies of theocracy, the millennialism, socialism, theosophism, and behaviorism for all of America for a better world.

Thomas More described an America Utopia in his works in 1477–1535. He imagined a Utopia would be self-contained, isolated on an island with like communities embracing a common culture or "way of life." Thomas More imagined his Utopia in which the citizens enjoy a near-perfect existence and experience perfect politics. Thomas More's Utopia is viewed through Thoreau's *Walden*. Thoreau's *Walden* begins with his introduction to Walden Pond. During his two years in Walden Pond, located in Concord, Massachusetts, Thoreau Walden was void of the complexities of life's usual routine. However, he did return from being an "isolationist" to a civilized world. Life, he exhorts to us, is to meet our lives and live fully.

Utopia has its origins in the philosophy of Plato's first work, the *Republic*. The *Republic* defines Utopia as a place that extols idealism—a society that emphasizes equality for all its citizens. It is a framework for building a government that would legislate for the citizens and establish means to deliver support for such a society.

Plato's *Republic* presents a model of an ideal society which was divided into two classes with two different standards. Standard views were construed as dystopian which is a fright of a society, to my chagrin, where a few people wanted to live (Martin and Ray, 125) and is predicated on a firm class system (Godwin and Taylor) and successors of royalty and Plato's "philosopher and king.

Nevertheless, in view of Plato's knowledge of the conflict of life in an ancient world, without ambiguity, as well as epistemologists as rulers, there was apprehension among the rulers who made possible for all its citizens to express concerns as to whether or not all citizens who held on to slavery would for the best of society.

Utopias in America began as experiments. The focus was to create a society as described by Robert V. Hine in his work *California's Utopian Colonies*—one in which the citizen's ideas of living were the same. They shared a commonality of beliefs and a foreseeing of an ideal society that made it acceptable to withdraw from the "main" and construct a new society. This idea was welcomed by groups of different ideologies, religious and secular members. The religious groups wanted a society with a religious base to build a utopian society. The secular groups place emphasis on a society built on ideas of a "utilitarian creed" as a way to create an ideal utopian society and have a cooperative life. The Shakers in the eighteenth and nineteenth centuries built twenty of these communities. The utilitarian creed (John Stewart Mill) where utility greed is simply stated, not complicated, and morals are at its core "the greatest happiness."

There is a connection between ethical and moral philosophy for both utilitarian and religious groups. They both have concerns with discipline as it relates to "good and bad," the moral duty, and obligation to society. They both emphasize happiness, and happiness entails love, but religious ethics focuses on the poor and the downtrodden, the weak and disenfranchised more than others. Religion stressed more on the reason and the psychology to discern right from wrong to make a moral judgment and the individual as opposed to individuals in terms of worth.

Therefore, it is traditionally more about "deontology" and virtue ethics. The emphasis is on the relationships between duty and morality of human action. A shining city upon a hill, a divine paradise, a light unto nations is how Robert Nesbit describes American Utopia in his work in *The American Religion* (reported in his March edition, 1987 issue).

America is said to be unique among western society. In its Utopia-touched origins, John Winthrop, along with his group of Puritans, came to Massachusetts to create a society of bible purity. "We must always consider that we shall be as a city upon a hill, the eyes of all the people are upon us."

Winthrop and his group derived this philosophy inspired from Matthew 5:14 and used as a basis of the new nation they were going to create. Perry Miller, in his work *Errand Ino the Wilderness* brought awareness of the first crisis in the new world when this dynamic and faithful Puritan were not the center of attention of all the people, and secondly, as time passed, their morals were no longer that of the sacred hill. Nonetheless, their desire for the utopian life remains and was reflected in much of their intellectual history of the seventeenth century. They were preoccupied with what things needed to be done to become Utopian. They realized that they had to convert to certain conditions, overcome weakness, and attain virtue, and over a period of a few decades, a significant change was achieved.

The Puritans, when arriving in Massachusetts, had their designs on creating a Christian city. It was not long before the oppositionists of the divine epic could ascertain changing from Puritan Christian to the American (Ernest Tuveson, "Redeemer Nations: The Idea of America's Millennial Role).

CHAPTER

2

The Protestant Millennial Movement

When Protestant millennialism was formed, logically, there came with it a need to find a new chosen nation or nations. If history is theodicy, if redemption is historic as well as individual, then they must be children of light and children of darkness, geographically, and the city of God and the city of the world should be susceptible of being designated on maps.

During the time of the "Great Awakening" with Jonathan Edwards, one of the most salient figures that embodied Christianity and Americanism with zeal included a "body of rights." The latter oftentimes penetrates treatment of the thirteen colonies. This treatment increased the hated role of being the subject of the British crown. America was by now the "city upon the hill" as seen by a significant number of the revolutionary American. Without a doubt, a single American, down to and including Ronald Reagan, has failed in any way to invoke the "Matthew image" as a support by *America: The Redeemer Nation*.

It was this awakening of redemption that gave birth to the *American Jeremiad*, lamenting for long periods of time. This is described as a unique kind of literature that began in Europe as a part of the Protestant Reformation. Its greatest strength and vigor were in America with its genesis through Puritan use and expanded to America. "Sacvan Bercovitch" was another written type of literary work that echoes cultural puritanism and *Jeremiad* lamenting that found its way into the heart of literary form.

The *American Jeremiad* (lamentation) is a kind of ritual made to work in concert to link social criticism to spiritual renewal, private identity, the changing signs of times to a more convinced metaphors, and discourse of a type of symbol for representation of what spiritual renewal is.

To argue that the *Jeremiad* has played a major role in fashioning the myth of America is to define at once in learned and historical terms, myths, and may clothe history as fiction, but it persuades in proportion to its capacity to help men act in history.

The *American Jeremiad* started as little more than a sermon but was changed by the eighteenth century. It is an issue that can be viewed in secular as well as religious terms in ardent support of America, the beautiful, and Christ as well.

The authors of *Jeremiad* worked exhaustively to tell the story of America, the "city upon a hill," and hoped and dreamed which at one time been damaged and dismantled in the Old World.

The *Jeremiad* told, with expressed emphasis, what was wrong with America. They revealed America's wickedness and the evils that grew in the course of America's short history; however, they did propose a program that could be followed by which America could transcend and regain its innocence that has been tainted.

In this framework of action, the conviction America had through a mixture of divine and historical reasoning become the conscience of the world.

CHAPTER

3

The Expansion of the Spiritual Resolution, the Newspapers, Sermons, Oration, Pamphlets

Historical study, novels, and state decree kept *Jeremiad* alive and thriving through the decades following the revolution resulting in a widespread of millennialism throughout the continuum of human thinking. Education joined in and helped prepare plans for this spiritual revolution. They reasoned that this would help bring humanity to perfection. Political and moral entities concentrated on the possible disturbance of "God's plan" expressing the urging of technology as a tool to "revolutionize the land" into the creation of a human divine. Paradise labor leaders discovered in the revolution a postmillennialism justification for trade unionism.

The thought of progress was based on a promise, a cardinal proposition of American utopianism historically grounded in both Greek's nationalism and millennialism. They forged ahead stating mankind had progressed spiritually, morally, socially, environmentally, and politically, no longer by John Adams and Thomas Jefferson but by Europeans such as Condorcet and Godwin. They had some thoughts about the founding fathers and that America was at the forefront of this human turn of progress. America cozied up to those who favored them and said nice things about them as the Tocqueville did at the onset of democracy in America and paid less attention to tourists that came occasionally like Dickens who was not impressed and further observed Mencken and recorded it in his native language (American language). The nineteenth century was perceived as an age of sustained profusion of honesty telling an absolute without a doubt as well as other expressions indicating an America that is already expanding the world.

Historian and philosopher John Draper conducted nightly meetings in which he elaborated at length on the progress of America. The progress of America was, as John Draper explained, based on natural law, and he likened it to the bodily growth that is inherent in human nature and held together by principles of a society in the absence of a specific law. "The American Utopia was in sum, a part of a natural provisions of cosmic physics."

When we speak of cosmic physics, we are essentially explaining how the universe works based on the building blocks of our being as it relates to energy, matter, space, and time and how they work together and in what conditions. Cosmos, in essence, is the universe and is frequently understood as an orderly, harmonious universe during the sixth century.

Ernest Block discusses Utopia as models; the three models are teleological, discursive, and horizontals. He explains the rationale of the implementation of Utopia in space. Block experiments that the horizontal is more inclined to be a theory more efficacious because of the infiniteness of outer space by humans. Block points to the work of Frederick Turner's frontier thesis (1893) demonstrates what an early horizontal utopian theory is. It also describes how "frontierism" suggests a continuation of the involvement in the challenge of environment to assure continuity of ingenuity; therefore, it maintains virtue but with a caveat to consolidationism—accepting this planet as the only planet fit for human habitation. Immanuel Kant's *Perpetual Peace* (1795) while being "the best" is profoundly flawed.

It seems that Block favors the philosophy of the frontierists of their being potential for outer space Utopias and feels this can be a panacea by giving impetus for continuing cultural development on earth.

Much has been written about American utopianism in *Paradise Now: The Story of American Utopianism* (Chris Jennings). *Paradise*

Now led us to the period of the eighteenth century. *Paradise Now*, like other Utopias, was an experiment observing differences to Shakers' simple living as opposed to modern times.

Erik Reece's *Lost Mountain* depicts the coal mining industry as the economic spine for which families in that region had to rely on for job opportunities. With the onslaught of new types of mining, some say a radical strip mining only takes a few men to work it to scoop out coal. Reece took a journey for one year so that "we can see firsthand how strip mines have sheared away the mountain to the top of Kentucky." *Lost Mountain* details how this beautiful countryside has been reduced to only a speck on a map which is no longer up-to-date and which no longer exists.

Yorke C.C (2016) "Prospects for Utopia in Space" in Schwartz J. Milligan, Tony (Eds), *The Ethics of Space Exploration: Space and Society* (Springer).

Jameson Mckay's observation of Utopia "is the years, Utopia has again changed its meaning and has become the rallying cry for left and progressive forces." The search for Utopia has always been a quest starting as early as biblical times and continues until today.

The English writer Aldous Huxley, along with his wife, wrote about the times they moved to a small community of Llano in the Mojave Desert north of Los Angeles. This town, as they soon discovered, was once the site of Llano Del Rio—a utopian socialist community which was established in 1914.

The mines of the once populated town brought to mind the farmers' poems about a traveler in the desert who finds a broken statue fell from its base and partly buried in the sand. On the pedestal of this statue was a boastful message: "My name is Ozymandia King of Kings. Look on my works ye mighty and despair."

Huxley, in his novel *Brave New World* found the hubris and boastful manner of Llano Del Rio's founders who thought they created a town that would change the world. Sadly, Hurley was not prepared to express his doubts about their ideas. He had only been in the United States for five years. There was not enough time to go into nativism, but if given time, he too could explain the depth of the American drive to come up with a plausible paradise. Utopia was defined by many older factions and philosophical thoughts as being a fantasy than paradisal.

A Utopia can and does exist in our American society today. Although the two concepts, socialist and capitalist, are at the forefront of our political debates between the two parties. There are those who believe in making health care for all affordable or free and education for all and many other social programs like social security and food stamps. Socialists feel that citizens should be responsible for themselves.

Capitalism and Socialism:
The Preface of 1869

> The inherent vice capitalism is the unequal
> sharing of blessings; the inherent virtues of
> socialism is the equal sharing of miseries.
> —Winston Churchill

This country from the beginning and more, especially for the last forty years, has become a laboratory experimenting with all kinds of socialism. Nothing has been set before us, and we hope to learn something from these experiments.

Socialism is defined as the distribution of wealth and was not received well by most societies. It is a belief that the distribution of wealth could prove to be an onus on the people. Socialism's belief is that of an egalitarian philosophy that there should be shared property and resources. The socialist "should not be an island unto themselves, but a part of the main." They value a society that works collaboratively with one another. Everything that is produced is a social product, and so anyone is entitled to share in it. A distribution of wealth should be shared by all its member.

This philosophy juxtaposes capitalism whose beliefs are rooted in "free market,"—individual choices where individuals have their say how goods and services are distributed. The socialists argue that this kind of thinking would lead to unfair practices and has the propensity to exploit those who are less privileged and give more power to the more privileged who could dominate society and invade the idea of equality of opportunity for all. Karl Marx and Friedrich in their manifesto of the Communist Party (1888) "The conditions of free development is the free development for all."

The socialists added a caveat taking into consideration that while the socialists believe in sharing, they do make some distinction on what not be shared. Items such as personal property and items is not public as viewed by Thomas More in his *Utopia* (1516).

Socialism was seen by many in a variety of ways. By the socialists, it's what should be shared and what should not be shared. This was met with disagreement in terms of the different ways of sharing goods and services and property. Centralist and decentralists are two factions who define their views, beliefs, and are quite similar to that of the socialist and capitalists. If illustrated by a Venn diagram, there would be an overlap in similarities. Socialism believes in the distribution of wealth in the form of goods and services, and resources for the people is provided for everyone.

The centralist was interested in property control in a central authority of an ilk. Decentralists based their decisions on the concerns of decentralization of public property with a couple of stipulations. The resources should be locally "at least lowest levee" and by those who are not affected directly. This has been a constant behavior throughout the history of socialism, a practical movement.

There seems to be a certain amount of schism between the two factions: Socialist and capitalist, can't say which is better for society. Capitalism believes in free market, and the government does not use economic resources as efficiently as it should. The Socialists looks to government to control goods and services. They look to government to improve the lives of people. Socialists believe that inequality is not good for the people. They believe in equality for all. The socialist's concern is in that of the "haves" and the "have-nots."

When we think about what our country is at the present time, it is a version of the short story by Ursula Le Guin's *The Ones Who Walk Away from Omelas*. It is an analogy of what our society in America is today. The citizens who are the "have-nots" are like the little child locked away from the regular population living in squalor conditions.

While the "haves" are living a happy and vibrant life ignoring those who are living in abject poverty. The citizens of Omelas began to feel guilty and realized much of their joy had been off the backs of this impoverished child, so they walk away. Where and why did they walk away? I say in our Utopian-American society today, they began to feel the meaning of human suffering and the seriousness of the injustices exacted upon the less fortunate. So little governance is needed

> If all men were angels we would not need government. Or if the hypothesis were offered us of a world in which Messrs' Fourier and Bellamy's and More's Utopia should all be outdone and millions kept permanently happy. On the simple condition that a certain lost soul on the far off edge of things should lead a life of lonely torment. What except, specific and independent sort of emotions can it be, Which would make it immediately feel even though an impulse arouse within a clutch at the happiness so offered; how hideous a thing would be its enjoyment, when deliberately accepted as the first such a bargain? (William James, 2012. *The Will to Believe* and *Human Immorality*, p. 133, Courier Corporation)

When we say walk away, is an ideology that alludes to developing a more willingness to compromise.

With the capitalists and the Socialists, you rid yourself of the notion of developing an individual or citizen because of racial differences, inequities in educational achievement, and every citizen has self-worth.

> The stone the builders has rejected has become the cornerstone. (Psalm 118:22)

> Built on the foundation of the Apostles and prophets with Jesus Christ as the cornerstone. (Ephesians 2:20)

> The community of the Giver had achieved a great price. A community without danger or pain. But, also, a community without music color or art and books. (Lois Lowry, *The Giver*)

The journey to a more perfect society will be ever before us. It is our ultimate dream. Since the beginning of the 1930s, Thomas More's *Utopia* is a pride of perfect harmony void of ills that plague human kind, politics, government, religion, free of diseases, wars, and a place that is more egalitarian.

No, we are not as naive as the eleven-year-old Jonas in *The Giver* living in a futuristic society that is pristine and sterile where there is no fear, pain, war, hatred and one in which everyone is respected and valued where everyone looks the same and behaves in the same way with little competition. Individualism is important.

Some argue that *The Giver* could be compared to the preamble to the constitution. That notion is debatable and denounced by our ancestors. But for some, they view *The Giver* as having some similarity in that both create a more perfect union of our society.

The Preamble to the Constitution was fixed to explain the intent of our founding fathers to form a more perfect union. One where the people are more amiable toward one another, enjoy certain freedoms, live in peace, and ensure protection through a strong military to maintain peace at home or abroad.

During the course of this discussion, the word *Utopia* is defined, and it is made clear that utopia means a place—an ideal place for humankind; environmentally, politically, and governmentally, analogies have been made further to define and explain utopias and those characteristics that characterize them. One such analogy was the garden of Eden—an enchanting, captivating, mythical creation symbolic of human time and experience and the metamorphosis from a utopia into a dystopia which in the beginning was a perfect society. Society, which began as perfect, would turn into an imperfect society because of sin and evil behavior.

CHAPTER 5

We can't, we shan't become dystopia. I never
thought it would get this bad I never thought
that the reestablishment would take things so
far their incinerating culture, the beauty of
diversity. The new citizens of our world will
be reduced to nothing but numbers, easily
interchangeable, easily removable, easily destroyed
for disobedience. We have lost humanity.
—Tahereh Mafi

"Every difference of opinion," Thomas Jefferson warned in his inaugural address, "is not a difference of principles." Even if he was addressing the country after an election as bitter as the one that put our current president in the White House, he was trying to quiet the noise generated between the dominant parties which is analogous of our country today.

Today's voters, just short of three fourth of registered voters, have poor social and political views and become the party of resistance to this president and this era of a Republican party.

Dr. Terry Lyles explained that "it is not what happens to us in life that defines us; it is our response to what happens." Dr. Lyle's *Back to Utopia* alludes to more personal things in our lives. For instance, searching for a better life that can easily be applied in the need to redirect our country's path on which we are on at the present time instead of the continuous lamenting over what is happening in our country today. He further states that we can help ourselves by rising up to the challenges we are confronted with each and every day and going back to Utopia is as simple as rising to the occasion.

Back to Utopia was written and designed to help with the personal challenges of today; challenges that are found today have become a dystopian. How can we go back to Utopia?

The election of 2016 should take us out of an ethereal trance so that before casting our votes, we think about what is real; we should not be overpowered by glittering language and promises that can't be realized or materialized. Empty promises are all we have had after two years under this current presidency. Look beyond the frosting. Rather, look what is inside, at what is underneath.

> Those who ignore history are bound to repeat it.
> (George Santayana)

America is much like a kaleidoscope as it relates to identity government, faith, and in our social diversity. America is a kaleidoscope resembling mosaic patterns of people with differing ideas and traditions which are assessed by communities.

When does identity politics with its styles and ideologies question our country's motto, "E pluribus unum"? Identity politics are centered around certain social groups which all of our attention is directed, especially those who share character differences.

"These are times that try men's souls" wrote Thomas Paine. These words are quoted from time to time occasionally in troublesome situations, and this is certainly apropos to these times. For the past two years, we have been living in tumultuous times—times that are different than the world has ever seen. It is a world with an unstable economy, conflicts of morality, and where much of the people don't seem to be concerned.

Are we really oblivious to what is happening around us? Have we adopted an attitude of what you don't know won't hurt you? To be ignorant will somehow release us from our responsibilities, and ignorance is bliss. If you don't know, you don't have to worry about the problem.

One questions the honesty and the moral uprightness of the American people when they elected a president who is so inept, a moral degenerate; these flaws were public during the campaign. His loyalty toward the Russian leader is mystifying.

> When a person shows you who they are believe
> them the first time. (Maya Angelou)

This president has divided our country and united the rest of the world against us. He is uniquely admired by the white supremacists; he is a pathological liar and con artist, but what is disturbing are his rallies that's always attended by thousands of people including children. I wonder if they are there for a political rally or a clan meeting.

He opens the doors to the haters who have a penchant for expressing their hate for Black and Brown people, the media, and his predecessors. This seed spreading of hate can fall upon the minds of the young, and hate can be cultivated.

> The children are our future and we should be
> preparing them for the world in which there will
> be challenges and changes, global and domes-
> tic to compete in the world of technology, age
> of information, cultural changes and differences
> and the need for respecting other cultures respect
> and honesty with spirituality.

A utopian America cannot stand. Where did we go wrong? And can it be turned around, or can we expect a dystopian America to be the new normal?

America, at its beginning, was like a utopia. Of course, it is common knowledge; nothing remains the same as an experiment. Experiments are based on a premise, a hypothesis. Normally, through a qualitative or quantitative method, the outcome should indicate if these changes are working or not working. There is a gap in our country, humanity wise. For some, they feel a humankind divide and feel that the wheel of injustices keeps turning, and the noise drowns out the cries of the poor, downtrodden, and the disenfranchised.

We shan't continue this dystopian path. We must continue to strive for a more perfect society for which our founding fathers strove to achieve. But it becomes disheartening to witness some of our institutions that we hold in high esteem crumbling under the weight of this corrupt presidency.

The Supreme Court was once viewed as pristine, sterile, and biblical—an institution one can rely on to right the wrongs fairly and without prejudice. Now it has been infiltrated by questionable individuals. A justice judge who sat on the court for decades, Justice Anthony Kennedy, overtly admitted he relinquished his duties as justice judge earlier than planned in order to give a president, whose reputation is less than stellar, the opportunity to appoint a replacement for him. Who can and did get a judge who will save him in case criminal charges will be exacted upon him?

Here's something extra:

A Delaware boy named Joshua Trump asked the school to change his name following bullying from the other children; after several attempts to enroll him in other schools, he was called stupid and was spat upon.

Make America great again. Yes, America does need to be made great again because its greatness is being eroded by moral depravity by an amoral leader supported by evangelicals. The greatness of America will not be realized again until we make America moral again.

CHAPTER 6

Whence We Came

Life lies behind us as the quarry from once we
get tiles and copestone for the masonry of today.
—Ralph Waldo Emerson

"Harken unto me, look into the rock once you
were hewn, and to the hole of a pit whence you
were digged. Look into Abraham your father and
unto Sarah that bore you: for I called him alone,
and blessed him, and increased him" (Isaiah 51:2,
*America—Look Unto the Rock Whence Ye Are
Hewn* by Kenneth C. Kemble).

From our early days, we came to accept the fact that America was
named after Amerigo Vespucci while some others thought America
was named after Richard Amerike, an overzealous supporter and
financier of the John Cabot Lodge explorer (1450–1498). But it is
common knowledge, based on history of earlier times, that America
is much older. There is a plethora of research into the age of America
starting from biblical times.

America is viewed as a new and mysterious "promised land
flowing with milk and honey" prepared by the Almighty and how
men and women fought through ominous conditions at the risk of
their lives; there were times when they lost their lives. Some came for
religious freedom, and some came out of curiosity. During the early

nineteenth century, the United States was looked upon as a *marvel* and wonder of the world.

> Our God had placed us above all the other nations of the earth, just as he had promised to do if we were obedient. (Deuteronomy 28:1)

Today when you look at America, it is no longer the place it started out to be; instead, it is more a dystopian country. All around, we hear news about some of the most adverse behavior in the land of the brave and the free. We are not brave and nor are we free.

We are in bondage—a bondage of our making as a result from moving away from God.

> And because of the abundance of lawlessness, the love of many shall become cold. (Matthew 24:12)

We have become cold and have lost our first love.

We, as people, have accepted all kinds of ills. Abortion amounts to murdering babies. It seems alright, but we have become a nation of infidels of the highest level. America should do some soul-searching by taking an inventory of ourselves and look into the mirror. Look into your souls, and you will see that we are not such a great and free country that God had intended for us. How much longer is he going to tolerate our evil ways?

> All like sheep have gone astray. (Isaiah 53:6)

We must return to God. We can rise up! When is America going to come to the knowledge that we might be on the wrong track? That we might not be adhering to our earlier principles? Not ever in the history of America had we had to question the legitimacy of our president or the normalcy of our election when our constitution has literally become obsolete. It has been put on the shelf by this president who leads with an eclectic style and has created a dynasty within the White House. His cabinet is mostly made up of family members, and our Congress seems unwilling to reel him in.

The inability for congress to exercise their duties is not only a gap but has widened into a chasm. The House and Senate are playing games with one another. The leading members in the Senate manipulate judges in order to get the ones that will rule in their favor. They are pitting one against the other. The conflicts between these two factions are hurting the country, and no progress is being made. It is much like "Nero fiddles while Rome burns."

The House's power is weakened by the Senate leaders' shrew ability to use laws of the past, to override whatever laws the House attempts to put forth. We are in a constitutional crisis. Subpoenas are ignored by those on the right by disregarding the House's power to order these subpoenas and documents when it is necessary.

> When the world is storm driven and the bad that happens and the worse that threatens are so urgent as to shut out everything else from view, then we need to know all the strong fortresses of the spirit where men have built through the ages. (David McCollough, The Course of Human Events)

In the course of human events, the decline of the United States is becoming a fact rather than just a mere thought. Poor leadership and moral decay have been at the core of this decline. We are confronted with a dysfunctional congress and government, climate change, immigration, health care, and imperialism as it relates to an outstretched military. We have become a nation of haters, bigots, racists, and xenophobes.

"A nation divided against itself cannot stand," Abraham Lincoln once said. Our country is so divided that it is hard to define who we are and what our founding fathers intended it to be. We have abandoned our loyalty as is repeated over and over again. "I pledge allegiance to our country, one nation under God, indivisible, with liberty and justice for all."

Doesn't our nation's motto *E plurbus unum* (In God we trust) mean anything? Do we really trust in God anymore? We are being led by ideologies of a leader who resembles more of a dictator transcending powers over and above his administrators. Congress is generating hopelessness and despair among the people, and congress doesn't have the ingenuity to address the situation.

We are less safe in our country while the leader continues his shadowboxing with Kim Jong Un and his brinkmanship with Vladimir Putin. This type of behavior has proven to be more posturing for photo ops and can be dangerous for the safety of our country by misleading the American people with lies. To make himself look strong, he announced that ISIS has been defeated and that building the wall is imperative and many more pseudo achievements. Honesty and trust are a powerful philosophy but not with this leader.

Most people are ignorant to the inequalities that exist such as free speech. For some, free speech has been muffled almost to silence. Inequities in education, taxes, and capitalism favoring the "elite" have changed the face of the America that the founding fathers set forth for us and left this country in peril.

The Declaration of Independence has been shattered, and our rights that were endowed to us by the creators of this document are no longer respected. The power to exercise our rights has been denied to the people by a destructive government. When this document was crafted by the creators, there will be a long history of abuse of power. The people's right and duty is to essentially fire the government. When the people are not able to exercise these duties, when the people's powers are weakened by a destructive government, the country is in peril. The people are the country.

Utopianism versus Socialism

Early utopian socialists pontificated on socialism and wrote extensively on Utopia and utopian societies. Fourier says poverty is a bane on society and is linked to other problems. Arguments have been made over the years and span the globe on utopian socialism. An ill in that everyone should be responsible for themselves, and if you don't work, you don't eat. Today, we have similar arguments in the idea that distribution of wealth is not Democratic.

Utopia to some viewers is synonymous to socialism and to some a dirty word, especially true of those on the left. They feel that those on the right are taking a big leap to bolster the idea of totalitarianism. Protagonists think Utopia is delusional; it is delusional to think of any place as a paradise but having a perfect world should be desired. Sometimes, we tend to think a perfect place is one where there is a perfect peace and harmony where everyone loves one another, but if this were so, a utopian society would be monotonous.

Utopian society is manifested in the government for the people and by the people and adheres to the constitution and respect and protect the people's rights of life, liberty, and the pursuit of happiness. Some of these rights include having an opportunity for equal education, health care, job opportunities, and to live in a clean environment where we may have a military to keep us safe in a country where immigrants are welcomed and respected as an asset to America and not a liability.

Another misconception about utopia is that it is a place where everyone gets what they want. This is considered an absurdity that's virtually impossible, but we could strive to make it as equitable as possible. Also, some citizens take a pejorative view of socialism. The Democratic candidates in the race for the presidency advocate socialism. Their platform focuses on free education, free health care, and food stamps for low-income families as a supplement to their livelihood. This most resembles a utopian society and one that embraces the distribution of wealth. Other considerations are for citizens who have worked a lifetime and have grown too old to work any longer and people with disabilities or mental illnesses through no fault of their own who are unable to work, should they be ignored and disposed of? A socialist or utopian would make compensation for these people and implement ways to accommodate their needs that are ever-changing for some and unfortunate for others.

The pursuit of happiness is founded on citizens to maintain a particular way of life which everyone can work to find happiness. Thomas More writes in his second work on utopia.

The commonwealth has one main objective that so far as public needs permit as much time as possible. It should be directed serving the body with a measure of devotion to the freedom and the developing of the mind; this is believed to be the essence of happiness of life.

What the egalitarian philosophy fails to acknowledge is that not every human considers developing higher knowledge equivalent to happiness. What happens to the citizens that are not so inclined to pursue happiness through higher knowledge but prefer just to lounge on a couch? The cultivation of the mind is not considered by everyone to be an ingredient to happiness. In the beginning of utopia, someone thought reasoning was a brilliant idea. That it should be the thinking of one or two that dictates what is right and what is right for every individual.

Herein lies the division of minds. Utopia becomes questionable when an individual has abandoned certain individual rights and can be argued, Is it utopia if the individual has to limit their rights? It's not only their rights but their thoughts and beliefs.

The pursuit of happiness is in essence eternal; as long as man lives, he will be searching for happiness and express what happiness is. To some, happiness may not mean the same as others. Most would say happiness is in occupying oneself in activities that will prove to be good for their overall well-being and to gain rights to material things and be able to increase one's spiritual and moral development.

Man is in constant struggle in the pursuit of happiness as demonstrated in Abraham Maslow's hierarchy of needs theory. The highest is self-actualization for which he teeters on. For this reason, man keeps seeking the ultimate goal. Maslow's theory of needs is a pathway for happiness through self-awareness and self-mastery as the search for happiness goes on and continues.

> One evening an old Cherokee told his grandson
> about a battle that goes on inside people.
>
> He said, "My son, the battle is between
> two 'wolves' inside us all.
>
> One is Evil.
> It is anger, envy, jealousy, sorrow, regret, greed,
> arrogance, self-pity, guilt, resentment, inferiority, lies,
> false pride, superiority, and ego.
>
> The other is Good.
> It is joy, peace, love, hope, serenity, humility,
> kindness, benevolence, empathy, generosity,
> truth, compassion and faith."
>
> The grandson thought about it for a minute
> and then asked his grandfather:
> "Which wolf wins?"
>
> The old Cherokee simply replied,
> "The one you feed."

CHAPTER 8

The Other Side of Black Mirror

"The rule of cynic San Nihilists has led us to a dangerous place. For everything from better health care to wind farms is declared intrusive big state meddling."

Everywhere these days are imaginary perfect societies, period, from folktales to science fiction novels to the lofty fantasizing teenagers saving the world. Writers of history have traced dreamers of a utopian society from Thomas More, who coined the term utopia, to Plato's Republic, to Bellamy's *Looking Backward*, Etienne Cabot's voyage, and the feminist version Sarah Scott's 1712 Bluestocking Utopia. These are the many attempts to describe Utopia.

However, when studying the Judeo-Christian account of human history, you will find that it began in Eden and ends in heaven. Politics as a concept in utopia has been tainted by the events that took place in the twentieth century. These events make it difficult to see utopian projects when everyone is thinking Stalin's Soviet Union. Many novels and futuristic writings have been written, and the genre consists mostly of horrific visions of social engineering gone wrong.

We know it's possible to make the world more just, kind, and generous. We've been doing this for years.

Europeans considered that we already live in a utopia citing that almost all infants lived to become adults, that the city streets are free of sewage, women own property equal to men, all children go to school, and at the same time can indulge in the satisfaction that the chickens are not being mistreated. What's more is that these innovations were all partly or wholly as the result of government action.

Many generations have endeavored toward utopia. We get fulfillment from everyday utopianism whether it is in helping a stranger with luggage, offer a seat to the disabled, or cook meals for a family in crisis. Each time you show appreciation for a kindness, you are demonstrating a widespread willingness to sacrifice for strangers. It is so widespread that the economics of the entire labor sector depend on it. Most people prepared to help a beggar; we brace ourselves when we see a stranger not because we are afraid and don't care but because we do care.

Still, we are accused of not being real; it is for show for selfish motives. They threatened that we may become a monolithic machine of repression when we work together. The role of the cynics and nihilists has led us to this place. Democracy is being eroded by demagogues around the world. The basic provisions for the poor are being denied to the people, and the worst of these is that we are in the middle of mass extinction that threatens life on earth. All the while, the world is dying, and the nihilists and cynics continue to shut us down. To them, trying to make the world a better place is lethal, and we exhibit false compassion, nothing more.

The time that this kind of thinking is dangerous must be ignored. There isn't anything shameful or naive and unrealistic in wanting a better world. We must abandon the superstition that every attempt to solve our problems ends in an Orwellian dystopia.

It has proven over the years through history that good intentions do not predict failure, quite the contrary. Without them, nothing has been achieved. We must allow ourselves to plan utopian schemes and, in a practical way, act upon them to make a reality.

> If we are to do better we must free ourselves to try. (Sandra Newman)

The other side of *Black Mirror*, the United Utopian States of America shows how the liberals who are in power affect the safety, independence, and the well-being of our country. It shows a notion that the liberals are working exhaustively trying to achieve but in so doing have destroyed the concepts of logic in their efforts to push further toward a perfect world.

America is looked at as a world leader, and to continue to be a powerful nation, there are things it should be aware of. There are things being done that jeopardize this possibility (e.g., banning drilling on domestic soil which will make US dependent on foreign countries). And by demanding soldiers fight sensitive battles, Liberals deny them ability to win wars; liberal politicians are trying to remove God from all aspects of society prohibited by the First Amendment. Liberal ideologies are sure to cause chaos and moral breakdowns to our country by excusing bad behavior by pointing at worst behavior. Liberals have proven themselves to be unfit as leaders and are grossly unable to keep this country strong enough to maintain respect and admiration for our country around the world.

Liberals are not always honest when selling their demands. He is invariably selling something that you don't want; he often tells you half-truths on any given matter, and what's more ominous is you must trust him with the security of our nation. What's even more devastating is if you ignore their effort to broaden their agenda; to ignore their agenda is to relent and let them become grounded in their agenda. If their idiosyncratic ideas are allowed to persist, it will be theirs. It seems their liberal thinking on utopia is asymmetric to what the meaning of utopia is but is what they think right for the people of America. Their utopia is more dystopian.

Renew American analyst, Fred Hutchinson, remembers when he was a young man. He knew that the left was for the most part deceptive, although it took a while for him to find out what was at the core of this delusion. As time passed, he came to appreciate how radical is the lie they believe and why it leads to more deception.

The ideologies of the left are founded upon romanticism. It held that progress is a surety and creates a path to a future utopia. The commonly held belief is that utopia is a fantasy and is fantasized as a romantic belief in a perfect secular future society—an earthly perfect society of man's creation, not by God. Liberals have been a staunch critic of utopia and feels that there has been contradiction and hypocrisy that always overshadowed utopian projects like Plato's Republic or the Gulag of Soviet communism, the killing fields of Pol Pot, and now the blood and sand caliphates of ISIS.

There is tyranny in the womb of every utopia according to French economist and futurist Bertrand de Jouvenel. This was reconstructed to read there is the possibility of a tyranny in the womb of every human project but rather alluding to the current presidential campaign contests by Akash Kapur. And it's a utopian project but rather one with ominous indication that a tyranny may be hatching inside and aims to be a Democratic election.

This is a dialogue between two intellectuals with like minds but with different beliefs on the constructs of utopian society and how the human is responsible for its creation in the world that we inhabit. Man lives in two worlds simultaneously—one of war (his choosing by nature) which all of life depends and the other through our choices and actions. We create a world of politics; through legislation, we can write our own laws and rules. This realm of freedom is in which we discover our human ability to create a world of our own choosing.

The discourse between these two intellectuals ends with a confession—one of their own belief in utopian thinking. One admits he studied the subject for two years and was a participant on an honors program for a program of social thought in an institution. One thing that I learned was that the world we live in is not a given, and we individually and collectively can transform it into reality; the quest to change our human created reality is worthwhile. Our endeavors is what utopia means to me.

> If Kapur is right and if the return to the Utopians is at hand that means that my kind of utopian thinking is making a comeback. (Jouvenel, Good News)

Utopia is seen through the eyes of different ones and mostly based on their experiences in what country they live in. Crevecoeur's representation of America is an example of what he thinks defines utopia. He believes that America is a land where everyone can achieve his or her wildest dreams. Families can be healthy and united. Poverty is nonexistent, and everyone has unlimited opportunities for development. He also believes that everyone in America can own land, and this can be made possible without having to ask for permission from the nobles. This image is too perfect to resemble the reality of America ergo is classified as a utopia.

Crevecoeur's description in his first letters show America as a place too good to be true through his eyes and contrasting his definition with that of his country in which he was brought up in. He sees America as non-divisive where various religions view philosophical an ideological practices as harmonious, and immigrants can assimilate and enjoy the benefits of a prosperous life for themselves and their families. If they work hard enough, they could become Americanized by becoming a part of American ethos and patriotism and being melted into a new race of men whose labors and posterity will one day cause great changes in the world.

Crevecoeur's letters were in some ways seen as contradictory and, at times, pivotal but always filled with excitement when drawing a contrast of life in America to his own country that he left behind.

Crevecoeur was most in awe of what America did in the name of freedom. The divide that exists between wealthy and royalty does not exist in America. We have princes for who we'd starve and bleed; we are the most perfect society now existing in the world. In the United States, everyone can be landowner's, and the neighbors work together in the pursuit of religious freedom. He especially admires the way in which people of different races from different parts of the world now live as one.

CHAPTER 9

Is Utopia Possible

Much of what is said about Utopia is found between the pages of literary works and are salient and profound. Unfortunately, all of America are not readers of literary works in which there is so much to be gleaned to enhance our knowledge of Utopia.

Utopia is possible whether it is revealed everyday through a society whose members are of a like mind who are willing to work to attain the highest degree of perfection or by having a government for all the people. Both of these instances should exist in degrees. Members of society will work together to achieve a common goal with a willingness to compromise without prejudice and a limited government, not one that stifles free speech but one that is concerned about the welfare of its citizens in every aspect of humankind.

But if we are content to set one kind of criteria, maybe Utopia is not possible. Utopia has to be flexible; this is important for changing times.

It is said that Utopia is possible but extremely difficult. We need to grow as a species as we are still in our infancy. Compared to the universe, there are possibilities when we are able to improve our standard of living for all humanity, with the threat of boundaries of nature, only then a society can be created—one that is not in fear of loss of basic needs. This will create a path for the education of our youths for tolerance and understanding.

In time, we can reach Utopia if we as a species can leave the past behind. We can start to look to the future if we look into automation and technology. It is of ultimate importance to teach the younger generation to work together not only for the sake of the earth but also for humankind. This will show the importance of working together as the only way for everyone and everything to coexist. We can say, without any seeds of doubt, that the idea of Utopia is possible. However, there's much work needed to be done before this can be achieved.

Let's imagine this for a moment:

> Imagine there's no heaven
> It's easy if you try
> No hell below us
> Above us only sky
> Imagine all the people
> Living for today... Aha-ah...
> Imagine there's no countries
> It isn't hard to do
> Nothing to kill or die for
> And no religion, too
> Imagine all the people
> Living life in peace... You...
> You may say I'm a dreamer
> But I'm not the only one
> I hope someday you'll join us
> And the world will be as one
> Imagine no possessions
> I wonder if you can
> No need for greed or hunger
> A brotherhood of man
> Imagine all the people
> Sharing all the world... You...
> You may say I'm a dreamer
> But I'm not the only one
> I hope someday you'll join us
> And the world will live as one

CHAPTER 10

A City Upon a Hill No More

Past presidents have portrayed America as the "City Upon a Hill." This title was given to America many years ago by presidents of this great country. America was perceived as a model of charity and decency where a dream of opportunity was everlasting.

The face of America was sought by many writers who would later pay a price for expression of their freedom of speech. They face genocide, slavery, and oppression, but the spirit of American exceptionalism was not shaken.

Langston Hughes—a poet who wrote "Harlem" and a critic of the country—wrote, "let America be America again the land that never yet been an yet must be."

"A City Upon a Hill" is a phrase taken from the parable of Salt and Light in Jesus's sermon on the Mount. In Matthew 5:14, he tells his listeners, "You are the salt of the world, a city that set on a hill cannot be hidden."

Used in United States politics, John F. Kennedy was inspired by John Winthrop. He said,

> I have been guided by the standard of John Winthrop set before his shipmates Arabella, three hundred and thirty-three years ago, as they too were faced with the task of building a new government on a perilous frontier. We must always

consider he said that we shall be a city upon a hill. The eyes of all the people are upon us.

It was true then and is true now. They are observing our government in every branch and at every level, national, state, and local. This was framed and abided by men who were sensitive of their great trust and responsibilities using the experience on the Arabella as an analogy of our great country on a voyage no less hazardous than that taken by the Arabella.

A letter: Wake Up America

This letter is to make America realize that they no longer that city upon a hill. That beacon of democracy that offered hope to millions over the years is now in crisis. We have leaders who are derelict in their duties.

The political compromise that had once been essential for our democracy has been overshadowed by partisan mediocrity. Wake up America, "we are no longer stood proudly upon that hill but in a damp swamp of partisan mediocrity." (Robert B. Davies)

The founding fathers would decry what the nation they created had evolved into. They would see an America that they would never have envisioned, and they would speak disparagingly about what it has become.

Washington, Jefferson, Adams, Madison, and their fellow founders were courageous patriots who put country above all else. They saw America as a nation with potential for greatness, but they had grave concerns over dangers that lie ahead as the young grow and spread their wings. The founding fathers would be very distressed as they viewed the America of today—a nation now beset by a myriad of very serious problems, most of them of its own making.

Every man, woman, and child would like to live in a better world—a perfect world which is described as one filled with perfect peace, happiness, prosperity, and equality for all. Should this kind of world be hard to achieve? Perfect society has been debated by clergy and scientists as to what a perfect world would look like. Despite all the efforts and attempts to create such a world, it has failed. Human beings have not been successful in creating this kind of world.

Sir Thomas More wrote a novel portraying a fantastic society he placed on an island and named it Utopia—shorthand for a perfect place.

Here's where the circular talk begins. Utopia means no place. It is Greek, the *ou* means "no" and *topos* means "place." More knew that the place he wrote about was imaginary. He knew that there was no place on earth where all humans live in perfect peace and harmony, living lives without fear of pain, stress, or worry. This is contrary to the fantasy thinking of some who have seen poverty, crime, hunger disease, war, and corruption. It is true; Utopia is nonexistent in this world. Why not? It is said because we are not educated. Some eighteenth century British philosopher Jeremy Bentham and James Mill believe that with universal education for all, serious social problems would be solved by the end of the nineteenth century. Unfortunately, it did not turn out the way it was philosophized.

The idea of divine law was not accepted during the nineteenth century. The revolt is against the supreme tyranny of the phantom of God. It is as long as we have a master in heaven, we will be slaves on earth; education, in this time, was said to be a threat to God's state and existence, and there would not be a need for either of them.

It was predicted that education would spread so rapidly that by the 1900s, the state would be unnecessary, and men would only obey the laws of nature. Unfortunately, these two intellectuals' predictions were proven wrong; the twentieth century did not bring us Utopia. Some of the harshest wars were fought in the first half of the century, and millions of lives were lost. The United States alone deployed 16,000,000 men, and World War I was the most devastating.

So it has been proven that time has no effect on creating Utopia. Or should we allow more time for humans to figure out how to do it? That is what Marquis de Condorcet thought in 1793: "No balance have been fixed for the improvement of the human faculties; the perfectibility of man is absolutely indefinitely the progress of perfection. Has no other limit than the duration of the globe upon which nature has placed us" (Durant, p. 243).

The Unwinding
The Inner History of the New America

We are all in this together has been fixed in place by every man, woman, and child for himself.

There were concerns that America is falling apart. The issues were not one of any particular issue but was painted with a broad brush and carefully laid out all that is wrong in America. America is not seen by some as the fruited plains with bombs bursting in air but rather with cynicism. So much has happened in America that has defaced its once image politically with bankruptcy and broken dreams and so much more so horrendous that it could not be reported by journalist and likens to an "eating cancel" eating away at the bowels of America. The distressed housing in Tampa Florida to Pharma and America is displayed as "where only fools and suckers who believe in the mythology of equality, justice, and apple pie." It goes——on to say more deplorable things and doubts about whether America can have a true democracy supported by capitalist economic systems and wondered what the founding fathers would say, think, or approve.

Ergo, the unwinding of the core principles of our democracy such as our social contract, our simple decency, our bill of rights, and all that are on the road for which we, as Americans, are unwinding.

Other works of George Pecker are riveting and get at the heart of the matter. He raises the questions whether it is possible to have a true democracy supported by a capitalist economic system and would the founding fathers approve? Would the founding fathers believe what is happening?

America is in a crisis and a state of erosion. It starts with our past presidents Barack Obama, George W. Bush, and Bill Clinton.

It dates back from the growth of the totalitarian terrorist state to the bank to private central banks in 1913.

The same culprits who are responsible for our country's erosion and causing the country to become a failed state are the leading politicians, bankers, and corporations with secretive longtime relationships with the Federal Reserve. These all plays a salient role in taking from America, actually stealing from America, and these operations are long and global. They are found at the core of committing high treason against the American people and United States Constitution that has gone on for a long time.

Mismanagement is not the culprit in America suffering. It is these acts of high treason and epic fraud that are being committed by the country's highest political leaders who are at the heart of this enormous conspiracy against freedom and the core principles the country is founded upon. The fact is America is being robbed and held hostage by a political clique. It is not a figment of one's imagination, and all these conspiracies are done in secret.

They feel that they are not bound by moral and legal rules. Lying to the American people has become the norm. Government officials feel they can commit crimes and act of satanic evil because they are enlightened beings who are doing what must be done to save human civilization from global collapse.

If this has been going on for thirty years, then we are seeing a country who for generations of ineptitude is culpa as well. It seems the American institutions of higher learning have failed our students. There has been some controversy over the years debating what should be taught, and should it be for individuals or the country. After thirty years and a certain group of people benefiting under the sleight of hand for avarice purpose, Edward O. Wilson wrote a book titled *Consilience: The Unity of Knowledge* where he unifies the four main branches of knowledge. This is linked to science and humanities which has been noted by all who have read it. The creativity is so immense.

I am suggesting that the way Wilson intellectualizes creation would be apropos for our approach to the rating of our education system. It could serve as a model for a curriculum for our students so that they may be adequately prepared to understand and deal with the "cabal."

A liberal arts program should focus on political science, economics, philosophy, psychology, and the arts for aesthetic purposes. Through the arts, one can hone their brain and pursue creative thinking. America cannot survive another thirty years of failed Utopia.

Humankind has for decades searched for a better world to live in that places peace, happiness, and prosperity above all else but have had no success. Why? One might ask. A perfect society has been discussed in many ways by philosophers and other factions for what a Utopia would look like. Despite efforts to create the perfect world, everyone so far has failed, then we should look.

Utopia: When?

With the popularity of Utopia, growing perspectives from philosophers are numerous. It has been argued from all angles: from nonexistent to is it possible and what makes a Utopia and if time plays a part in creating this perfect world.

One such perspective is a device to create a better world for everyone. Some would like to see a longtime future for our world for today and for tomorrow, and this can be achieved in a short amount of time; others have speculated. To quote one philosopher, "I think that utopia social order if not vastly improved social order. Social order compared to what we have today could very well be possible within our natural lifetime say a generation or two."

It is believed that education is key in creating that perfect world. How important it is to be aware of self. How they live their lives. People should live their lives in the best possible way. Education can augment humanity to a higher state not limited to technology but intellectually, morally, and culturally. Building a healthy body creates a healthy mind which is basic to human endeavors, and it is a belief that this can be achieved without stress. The question now is how?

Any building or creation tools are needed whether it be a blueprint, software, or hardware. It is suggested that the use of mass modern-day technology and the Internet is an excellent way to disseminate information and educational processes; it is also a way to gather people as many as possible to collaborate and discuss an issue or topic.

Man has to visualize and create a "mind movie" of the world he wishes to create. The current state of the country including global warming and what could be insurmountable conflicts have overshadowed man's hope for that peaceful and perfect future that it still can be realized in the distant future. And this tells us not to be dismayed. Challenges should not be viewed as rendering us hopeless. Challenges can bring about change. "Out of bitter comes sweet" (Judges 14:14). Sebastian Mercier during the French Revolution wrote, "Force and courage belong to the people of this earth. Happy are all the people who by information or by instincts sees the crisis." History makes aware that there are people like Mercier who dreamed of a better world and made attempts to make it happen.

Sometimes, man does not always use the uniqueness of his brain effectively and therein lies the root of the problem. The brain is where all of life experiences are written, and these experiences influence human behavior. There were flaws in the way man handled the global conflicts. He pursued short-term gains with little regard for future stability. In his eagerness to obtain immediate gratification, he lost sight of the value of long-term rewards. Man is said to be a creature of habit, and the fact is that temporal gains stems from man's innate instinct that was used during the prehistoric times. When the hunter killed the prey, he felt he had to eat all of it in fear that he might not get again.

Despite our seemingly awkward behavior when it comes to short-term gains, we were able to achieve long-term rewards. Inhabitable land survived winter, and we grew crop harvests and all the while growing a mature society because of our brain even though we humans don't understand how the brain works.

When we understand our strength, we can capitalize on them; when we understand our limitations, we compensate for them. Knowledge is a powerful tool to create a better world to improve our times and the world's.

Is Utopia More than a Dream?

In man's eyes utopia is a dream but a dream that can be realized if only we were to adhere to the laws that govern the universe; utopia is viewed by man as an ideal world—a kingdom of God which is trumpeted in all dimensions of our world. It is one in which an individual conducts his life in the best possible way by practicing and upholding the truth and therefore, rightly dividing the word of truth (2 Timothy 2:15).

This dream can be realized and is founded on the individual. Utopian dream is individualistic and cerebral in that everyone has to be cognizant in every way of the way he lives his life. Daily practicing of the truth is cerebral in the way that he thinks or not thinks. If the individual can overlook the peripheral as it relates to his environment and other entities surrounding him, it can help him achieve this true heaven on earth.

> Creating a utopia begins with the principle of the mind and teachings about the mind. (The Science of Happiness)

First, in order to create an ideal world, there are three guiding principles that we must follow. These are in the areas of institution of spirituality, economics, and research. The number one principle is to establish spirituality. The age of spirituality is the age of majority of people with like minds who are willing to accept the truth about the law of reincarnation. When the age of spirituality is instituted, mankind will understand that the crisis the world undergoes is designed for our soul training.

The second principle is economic reform. This entails profit management. Profits are to be used to meet the needs of the people and suggest that the economy lean toward worldly values and the values of truth. The economy and world values should join together collaboratively to show the will of God to bring about unity. "In all things acknowledge him, he will direct our paths" (Proverbs 3:6). The economy should be sufficient for the here and now.

The third principle is to conduct research and institute two more major principles. Each individual will learn by studying the truth and inquiry into the right mind. Each person should be able to create his own personal utopia which could ultimately lead to a personal fulfillment. If each were to work toward the attainment of happiness and create a utopia at home, some small units of utopia on a national and global scale would lead to a transformation of society thereby creating a world of peace and harmony and prosperity.

> If the world is filled with people who truly care for those around them the world will automatically become a utopia. (*Change Your life, Change the World*)

The Anatomy of Discontent

Discontent is defined as dissatisfaction of mind or unquiet in mind through having one's desires unsatisfied or thwarted. While this can be true, the question remains, is it enough, or does it go far enough? Freud, a well-known figure, is of the same opinion as Hollander who is a clinical researcher and has spent most of his stellar career dissecting an anatomy of discontent that reaches deep in the recesses of modern souls. However extremely personal discontent is, it makes its way out into the political and social arenas. The condition of being, it never finds rest; it always uncovers or invents new injustices, new moral outrages to sustain itself. I find these observations to be a link to man's discontent with respect to find his utopia.

This will probably be with man forever, and it may be a good thing in that it keeps people thinking and criticizing. Skeptics, as a result, can reach down to the recesses of man's soul and raise man's consciousness about his surroundings, be it environmental, political, economic, governance, or spirituality. Utopia is not a prejudiced term. It is a process to build a better world for all. To build a society that is more just and offers a brighter future for all. This can't be more true than it is for the Black community in the present day leftover from slavery. After the emancipation, the word *separatist* was coined because they were perceived by the white race as separate and not equal to them. The Blacks felt isolated and unaccepted as part of the human race.

Most recently, reparation has been revisited, supposedly to make up for the injustices imposed upon the Blacks during slavery. It would be difficult to erase the longtime indignities Blacks suffered. Rather than being oppressed by the white culture, which deemed itself superior, Blacks should have a utopia of their own.

> We all are humans until race discriminate us, religion separate us, politics divide us and wealth classified us. (*Palm Beacher*)

Black Concept of Utopia

"To unify collectively under one mind in order to build a nation of their own." What is Black Utopia? I feel to quote verbatim:

> Black Utopia so as not to weaken the intent or have the reader misconstrue their intent. A collective of like-minded individuals whose minds are in agreement under the foundation; Sharing the same visions that they see as Black Liberation. It's production of all resources which includes but not limited to food, water, transportation, clothing, healthcare, security, education, politics, etc.
>
> A village where order and structure are present. Where we control our own government; we elect our own officials in office who properly represent us and hire police that properly serve and protect our sovereignty. How will this come to existence? By collectively working together in required operations. Effective recruiting methods and pulling together of resources, education

and qualifications to form self-independence. Spreading the idea of Black utopia to likeminded masses and collecting monthly dues, sales and donations to raise finances.

Complete cooperation from all utopian citizens who will receive legal protection from the said government and military protection from alien threats. Well managed systems of government to ensure proper representation and structure by putting race first over petty differences in order to create divine unity amongst us. (Utopia: The Endless Search)

Politics and Economics: One Step at a Time

The search for utopia will be ongoing for all of humanity. It has piqued the interest of mankind spiritually, intellectually, and philosophically. There is no one answer given, at least in part, of what utopia would look like. Utopia is viewed by many as being man's ultimate dream to have a society that is perfect or almost perfect. It would be a place where all of its citizens' needs will be met, and they can feel a sense of meaning for each individual.

This sounds ideal and possible in some ways. It is in the implementation that problems could arise. Utopia may be difficult to achieve, and the thought of the inability to achieve utopia can lend men constant frustration which is demonstrated in the writing of Paul Hollander's "Discontent and Dissatisfaction." Hollander writes that "when anxiety reaches a certain level it can cause frustration and lead to perpetual state of unfilled longing."

There is a dark side of utopian theories that bear overtones of communism. It is when some utopian theories favor the need of a group rather than the individual which have been persecuted in the name Utopia.

The word *utopia* has come to mean more than the simple ideologies held by the first Puritan settlements whose main goals were simplistic and espousing Christianity as the years pass. Utopia has raised the consciousness of man in the areas of government, politics, economics, and of other cultures. Afro-Americans, Native Americans, and others reminisce over terrible injustices that were imposed on these citizens. The term *utopia* has stretched over all the world and societies as being a place of peace and harmony with no risk of disease, war, and other pestilence that can plague man. It is more or less viewed as heaven on earth. When this seems to be unachievable, man becomes more determined to keep searching. Somehow deep down in the recesses of man's soul, there is a utopia that can be achieved.

Spirituality of Utopia: What Does Man Seek in His Life?

Jesus is the life in this world and the next, period. The reason you cannot see what you are seeking for is that you are separated from him.

The mystification is what makes us human. It is an age-old question for which many answers are given, although they may be varied in some instances. Man, during the early years, explored his uniqueness through his creative abilities using tools. Today, man is defined in terms of innate spirituality. It is said that man's struggles with years of pain and suffering can only be responded with hope—hope to find an earthly paradise.

Is a spiritual utopia possible? Yes, the scripture describes the possibility of experiencing the peace of God that passes all understanding and peace just like a river and righteousness like the waves of the sea (Isaiah 48:18).

The Bible teaches us much about God's plan for humankind after this life here on earth. But God has in no way promised mankind a place in heaven. It is only a variation of the dreams of utopia. The Bible speaks to us in scripture and verse. For example, whatever man thinks about life after death, there is no pie in the sky after you die; the grave is not an open door to the life beyond (Psalm 6:5; Ecclesiastes 9:10). But when God returns, and he will return, he will give a permanent new life to his people (1 Corinthians 15:22–23). Together they will set a just and beneficent government of perfect service on the earth for a thousand years (Revelation 5:9–10). The scenarios depicted in the Bible are very real and a very real practical world which mankind is welcomed and can live forever (1 Corinthians 15:12–24).

> They shall beat their swords into plowshares and
> their Spears into prong hooks nation shall not lift
> up sword against nation, neither shall they learn
> war anymore. (Micah 4:3)

The United Nations dedicated this as their objective. God's plan for his people were from the beginning here on earth and beyond.

The Bible teaches all about God being omnipotent, omniscient, and omnipresent. His powers and goodness have no limitations. He wants us to search for these practical and real utopias.

CHAPTER 12

Ethics versus Religion: A Debate

Can we be ethical without being religious? Can we be one and not the other? If we were to analyze the two, we would find that there is built in most religions a certain amount of ethics. Ethics do play a role in religion. Ethics is a major branch of philosophy to include right conduct of good life. It may stretch a little further to include right, good, and duty.

The core aspect of ethics is the good life—a life that is worthy of living and one that is satisfying. This is the opinion of most philosophers going back to ancient Greece. Happiness was achieved through one living one's life in accordance to virtue. *Virtue*, in a real sense of the word, will allow adult individuals to not just involve good personal habits but also friendships and intellectual virtue. The essence of virtue holds dear what the holistic view of Plato and Aristotle shared in the third and fourth century about integrity. Immanuel Kant has a belief that the idea of God is the basic requirement of ethics. Kant believes that a man should be virtuous and accept his responsibilities in order to be rewarded with happiness. Kant feels that virtue in this life is not often rewarded but is reserved for the life beyond and a God to see that it is so.

We have many kinds of religions and just as many seem ambiguous when it comes to following rules. However, there are some rules that are not clear and can be difficult to follow. Albeit, Scriptures is God's Word, and God's Word cannot be changed nor voided. God's Word and commands must be followed with no ambiguity.

When moral decisions are contemplated, what part does religion play in making them? America tends to characterize some individual's religious beliefs and renders them incapable of making ethical decisions. Ethical sentiments cannot be made without the influence of one's religious beliefs; our most basic sentiment is linked to our religious ideology.

In the meantime, we do consider religion as a basic code of guidance, more or less, a handbook to keep us in line. There can be some differences based on different ideologies that most have gained through our social institutions and can affect our decisions. For example, most people agree that things like murder and adultery are always wrong regardless of the circumstances. Man, since the beginning of time, has been a complex specimen—a specimen that philosophers, social scientists, and scholars around the world have been trying to understand the nature of man and how he thinks. We have now come to succumb to the use of semantics to define mankind.

I do not wish to offend our most renowned philosophers such as Kant, Plato, Aristotle, and many others of our twentieth century philosophers; as some might say, it is sacrilegious to criticize these wise minds. These are the giants whose shoulders we have stood on for centuries and who are so close to spirituality. Such terms as ethics, virtue, morality, and integrity cannot be considered a part of religion; otherwise man would be considered an infidel.

God is our creator; he made the whole of us. He knows what we need: that of a sound mind, a conscious intellect; we can explain the universe. He has enabled us to see through the study of arts, literature, and science to show his handiwork throughout the natural world and psychology so that we can understand ourselves and others of our world.

Utopia remains throughout the long history of the world, the basic narrative of a journey. First comes the picture of a happy people in a beautiful and well-ordered setting then comes the lecture on how it all came about, how it works, and by implication, how it might be made to work in the traveler's own society.

Here's a look into how the idea of utopia exploded into social and political actions and explore into which ways this idea could be realized: at the outstart, utopia was more or less limited to the idea of social environment, period; since then, it has shown itself in many more ways. The idea of world peace was seen as utopian, and utopian communities sprang up all over the United States.

We went from the simplicity of living as the early communities lived by sharing resources with one another to developing social ideas to an ecological utopia with concerns for nature, to economic utopia which began in the eighteenth century. This turn of events caused the development of commercialism and capitalism combined with socialism. Lastly, a religious utopia is contained in both inter and intra religions to include the scientific relating to the standard of living; with this objective, an approach to the idea omit death and human suffering of all kinds that is inevitable during a lifetime to make the human condition perfect.

Technology utopia will replace human needs in the future. Technology will be utilized to benefit human quality of life so that humans can enjoy a higher quality of life.

A constitution was written as a framework by which a set of laws are established for the interests of the people to ensure the people's safety and domestic tranquility as is deemed by the preamble to the constitution—to provide for social justice for the infirm and the weak and for those who are suffering hardships.

The early works on utopia and utopianism is predicated on the various ways that people perceive what a perfect society should be and borrowing from the philosophical underpinnings of our psychologists and ethicists and other factions of society. This constitution was written by Sir Thomas More which was inspired by his first book on utopia and how utopia was visualized at the outset.

> It seems to me that where private properties exist where all men measure all things in relation to money it is hardly possible to establish in public affairs, a regime at once just and prosperous, unless you deem it just that the best things belong to the worst person. Or unless you judge that all goods be shared among the fewest people

however they are not entirely satisfied. While also others are in direst poverty. This is why I reflect upon the constitution of the Utopians, so morally irreproachable among whom with the fewest possible laws all is regulated for the good of all in such a way that merit is rewarded; And that, in sharing from which no one is excluded everyone has nonetheless a large part. (Thomas More)

CHAPTER 13

Utopia: A New Era

It was in the 1930s that photographer Jason Reblando, while documenting public housing units in Chicago, discovered what he called intriguing but little-known phenomena in history. Three Greenbelt towns were established in the 1930s as part of the new deal program. They were planned, built, and managed during a period of President Roosevelt's New Deal project.

Reblando took a different approach to tell his story of this obviously unique history of these little towns through pictures. The focus of this program was developed by the resettlement administration, the president's right-hand men and part of his brain trust. Tugwell was named as the overseer of the resettlement administration or RA. The aim was to resettle people who were losing their farms and homes and those who are living in urban areas.

Tugwell saw land on the outskirts of a metropolitan area, and he named it the new frontier. He saw this land as prime property that's ideal to build suburban settlements. There was a lot of thought that went into this project. Tugwell was to design garden cities inspired by a British urban reformer named Sir Ebenezer Howard. He was taken aback by the overcrowded situation in London. He saw the problem and was willing to solve it. After giving it some consideration, he thought decentralization of cities and communities would be a solution to this problem. Decentralization outside these huge metropolitans would offer the people the best of country living with social advantages of living in a community where people can enjoy fresh air and be given space that is part of the country.

Jason used his camera to photograph each of these little towns. He used a 4x5 camera to capture the images of these towns. He was inspired by his curiosity, and the residents welcomed him. He was enthralled over these three cities including Greenbelt, Maryland; Greenhill, Ohio; and Greendale, Wisconsin, and their history and visual appeal. He worked alongside historical societies. Many who had the opportunity to observe this unique but quaint little "cities" admired the basic concept of the Greenbelt that borders the community. They weren't built too close but not too noticeably away from the metropolitan area that bordered control to towns growth and have nature built into the residence; interaction was deemed to be looking forward look ahead.

The New Deal legacy was to create a place conducive to humanity and want that the residents felt a certain kinship with others. The planners detailed every aspect of human existence as if they were going to live there themselves.

Jean Card writes on dystopia: "By Government-Big Media. How the two are dominating America's Society and suffocating free speech; asking the question "who will rise up. Who will speak up?"

It is sensed that America is beginning to resemble pages out of futuristic-written book. What with the continuous activities by the jihadists at an epic proportion. The atmosphere resembling Armageddon, global warming (climate change), the economy being exponentially dysfunctional, and culture changes in politics that are currently taking place in politics seem to be increasing in its momentum. Layers of culture resembles that of "tectonic plates" causing an upset in people lives and is still present as we speak.

Card paints a picture of a dystopian society, and we all should be concerned about it as it is becoming more real; many novels have been written by futurist. One would wonder if we are at a prequel a do-over today.

Small businesses are practically all gone away; only corporations are working with big government. Technology is almost unrecognizable because of its advancement that's so fast that it seems almost magical.

Our source of information is centralized; the oppressed have to fight for things that are supposed to be rightfully theirs as afforded by the constitution.

Our current government is remiss in its duties—a lack of ingenuity to function rationally; we legislate under partisanship and leadership that serves to delay progress of the country.

This story is just a look into history, a place in time. At this time, a project was a model for how a nation should think about themselves in this plan of egalitarianism, and cooperation may seem against the principles of rugged individualism and capitalism. Albeit, this program has brought about means that turn to improve people's lives during the Great Depression, both socially and economically. I think we all can truthfully say that we hope and pray that our country will not ever have a Great Depression again. I hope we can look at our fellow citizens and think the law of sunshine and let the sunshine through.

> You must love beyond the differences of all religious nations and races. (Ryuho Okawa)

Another story chasing utopia was told through a film during the 1920s. The story is told about immigrant Jewish workers living in the slums and ghettos. They managed to lift themselves out of impoverished conditions by combining their resources and building what is referred to as co-ops. With these resources, they were able to buy and operate their own complexes in the Bronx. They believed, as homeowners, they would be better off to control one's fate and one's future.

In *At Home in Utopia*, the united workers cooperative colony was the center of interest; this group was also known as the coops which the more common people and members were the operators of this Jewish labor-housing coops and was populated mostly by sympathizers to the communist movement.

This movement began as a secular European working class of people of all different races sought to instill their purpose-driven ideologies as part of the international movement; as a community, the co-ops provided the residents with all the things they had dreamed of in their adopted colonies. It considered all the aspects of human life that humans need for their emotional and educational and spiritual well-being and the environment as it relates to spaces. The people should have green space for gardening, space for sports, and play areas for the children and also community spaces for meetings, dances, recreation clubs which flourished, and a library of twenty thousand volumes written in Yiddish Russian and English. Most importantly, since they were essentially skirting the progressive reforms that would be sure to sweep the nation as part of their progressive underpinnings, the co-ops invited African Americans into their complex fostering lifetime friendships and even interracial marriage; they, like the New Deal project, wanted to provide for the people a living that was needed for mankind.

This movement during this period of time in the 1930s was to bring their passion for racial injustices and felt that this could be better achieved by integrating their own cooperative housing. Though met with some unexpected consequences, it was found that this age-old tale of the struggle for equity and justice spanning two generations were seen to have ups and downs.

There is tyranny in the womb of every utopia waiting to be born. This is illustrated in the film about the rise and fall of one community. For the 1920s into the 1950s, there was emphasis in the passion that bound us together to those that tore us apart. But as we follow along the paths, *At Home in Utopia*, it can attest that living with courage across the barriers of race, nation, languages, conviction, and sometimes even with common sense is possible.

At Home in Utopia captures the epic struggles across two generations as the coop residents experiment with breaking down barriers of race and ethnicity and champion radical ideas that would transform the American workplace.

How the World Is Shaped by Utopia

Since the idea of utopia was introduced by Thomas More, there is now an economic utopia, a political utopia, a social utopia, and an environmental utopia, each highlighting their creation of a utopia and how they purport to accomplish it. Utopia thinking has asserted itself in all walks of humanity.

Visions of utopia was experienced in the Christian world when it had its beginnings when the colonies during the sixteenth century were in search of this perfect place to realize their vision. But recently, all visions have been hung in the balance arguing politics and religion and how America is in decline and if there is hope for America yet.

America, for ages, has been showcased as a place of opportunity and hope—a place which has been sought out by people from all over the world as a source to help them realize their dreams. But to their chagrin, they did not find this as truth. They could see how families were tom apart because of the uncertainty of employment and financial problems that a family unit might face. The family unit might also breakdown by infidelity and divorce. With all the realities of this ilk, one must wonder if there is hope for America.

> No one political party can fix America only God
> can intervene and bring back America.

On the other hand, Christian utopia envisioned a government of Christian laws and morality in their attempt to escape from an oppressed Europe by making their way to the new world. They did not use the church to propel them to this utopia that they wished to create and keep but through American political systems which they believed was guided by the hands of a Christian God. An aberration from what was believed to be Christian political social order was viewed as evil, ungodly, and even satanic. Often branded as Liberal, they looked upon Liberals negatively.

Politics and government in themselves are not evil; in fact, they are established by God himself. Romans 31:1 says, "Only when they are used to replace that which the church should be engaging our society, then it becomes evil."

Society in Denial

Comparing America today with the 1950s and the 1960s when America was admired around the world for its richness in economics, military prowess, and cultural advantages. But recently, America is seen in decline, and society is in denial. The people are sensing that something is wrong. The most concern is for the increase in socio-economic inequality and the dwindling of our national identity and purpose. America is viewed around the world, and they worry about their children's future; will they be as prosperous as we are? Society is in denial. They have developed the ostrich syndrome, "stick your head in the sand."

We are on the eve of destruction; is there hope for America? God has been our every hope and stay. He is forever teaching us in the way we should go; to receive everlasting life with him beyond this world, we should be concerned about our country heading down the wrong path, but society is in denial. Do we not feel a sense of urgency deep down to examine ourselves and come out of denial and face the realities surrounding our country's future? With moral decay and political and racial unrest, we have much to do.

Maybe we have generated this kind of feeling and behavior because our leaders are in decline. Despite the fact that we are a Christian nation, it is being dispelled by some of the most forceful factions; these are the media who gobbled up the lion's share in reporting everyday news that might be true and sometimes unreasonably confusing as well as special interest groups with campaign promises. They have all made their goal to eradicate all indication of Christianity from public life.

The founding fathers would be appalled to see America today. To see the nation that they created has turned out to be the nation they never envisioned: the kind of America it is today. When they created this country, they could see greatness while expressing their feelings of ambivalence over dangers that lie ahead as this nation grew and spread its wings.

If they were to see America today, they would be very unhappy and grieved over the abundance of problems that the country is faced with today, much of our own making. They would be especially concerned about the imperialism our country is engaged in, the overstretched military, endless wars, and the economic and cultural struggles of the United States.

American Resiliency: Bounce Back from a Great Fall

Historically, the United States has been known for its resiliency. We have been through a Cold War, terrorism, nuclear threats, floods, the Great Depression, and now an opioid crisis and much more, and we have come back from each.

> One generation grows trees; The next generation
> will enjoy the shade. (Ancient Chinese proverb)

Each generation embraces the next generation by giving hope and optimism. But we have met the challenges of high technology and its effects on the lifestyle of the people. We need ingenuity and resilience to bounce back from the past two years.

Never in the history of our country have we had to question the legitimacy of our president or the normalcy of an election. The meaning of the constitution seems to be shelved and obsolete, and those who lead by an elected system and Congress will not call him down; this paper tiger president is uniquely and fundamentally unfit for the office. He does not let truth get in his way. His behavior displays that of a dictator and a despot. We cannot feel safe in this country when he fires all the generals who are critical for overseeing foreign affairs and military exercises; all of which are essential for keeping this country safe.

> To be prepared for war is one of the most effective
> means of preserving peace. (George Washington)

In the first few months after coming into office, he fired all of his aides who would not express their loyalty to him and do not lend themselves to his idiosyncratic behavior. This president's approach to the office of the presidency is the exact antithesis to previous presidents for decades past. It is strange in the way that he tweets insults to anyone who says something about him that he does not like; he gives juvenile and often offensive nicknames to those who criticize him. He has half of his staff mesmerized and the other half terrorized.

Granted, we have undergone in recent years some major, if not catastrophic, events in our country that threatened to shatter our democracy. Albeit, America will rise again and rebuild again.

To rebuild America, our first thought immediately is about our political system, economic infrastructure (roads, bridges, tunnels), our military, and a congress who seems to have turned their attention elsewhere other than facing the country it is confronted with to rebuild our country.

While these are salient to the building of America, we need to be an inclusive country. There is not a liberal America and a conservative America; there is only the United States of America. I will venture to say America has to embrace all of America. Our country has been polarized based on racial discrimination and our view on accepting immigrants. America is a melting pot made up of many races, cultures, and creed, and they all contribute to the greatness of our country.

We need to come together collaboratively and discuss where we are and to make the changes where needed and how we think or view our country and how we are viewed by other countries. A return to a utopian society has been intimated; however, this raises the issue of socialism which, to most Americans, is a bad word. Just recently, our politicians have been campaigning on free education and Medicare for all and come under fire by the nonconservatives.

In early years, a socialist system was instituted whose motto was to each according to his need. This was the early socialism. In the 1930s, this philosophy was extended over from according to his need to according to his ability (the young are more able and fit for labor service). They complained about being forced to spend their time and strength to work for other men's wives and children. This form of socialism was short-lived and was soon abolished. At the same time, America was strong enough to overcome the atrocities and conflicts that the country had to endure and build the country like physical environment and like political environment. We as America will be prepared to quiet the noise.

> We the people are one with the power apropos to
>   rebuild America: a poem
> our opportunity to shine is dawning at this hour
> we are preached about a future containing hope
>   and change, but by definition of those
>   words make seem strange,
> our founding fathers worked hard in its creation
>   to see our change at its foundation,
> they make faulty plans to aid in our health and
>   feel that workers should share their
> wealth,
> those who work hard to pursue the American
>   dream are paying for those who do not
> try, it seems
> its sneaky plans and shady deals that much as lose
>   the trust me we feel

71

and when the nation tries it just power and dis-
arm it becomes frightening and they're
looking to harm
but for our country there is a chance to better our
lives and nation enhance
it is in times that we feel so lost and broken that
we must hear the words unspoken
each one of us is touched with the silent call is
take a rise and prevent our fall
For those of you who work so hard I promise that
you will make it far
even when truth seems scarce we shall pursue it
also fierce!

A Return to Utopia:
A Vision for a Perfect World

Without vision, the people will perish. Visions are essential for humans to have life; without vision, people would cease to exist. The human is unique in that there are two sides to us, and each of these sides have needs; it is important that these needs are met in order for the human to develop holistically. These sides are the mental and emotional sides of us that need a feeling or sense of purpose and a sense of meaning to shape a dream to nourish and pursue; there is also that physical side of us that needs the environmental elements such as sunshine, air, water, and food. Our religion and our civilization distinguish us from other kingdoms and a central realization of that perfect vision to pursue.

Man's secret for a perfect vision without a doubt has been long and enduring. There are all kinds of utopian visions that have swept the earth time and time again. They have in the past been referred to as movements much like those started by Buddha, Lau Tsu, Confucius, Abraham, Mohammed, and Jesus where millions of people gathered; they underwent centuries of unrest and many times hostile changes, and there were others that were more or less like shooting stars, flashing and then vanishing forever.

Observers of these movements leave them in awe at the determination of humanity and the continued repeating of this determination again and again; two essential mistakes were thinking that each vision was the one that would be a solution for all humanity's problems, and secondly, others must believe that this is the one true vision of humanity and need to follow. The need to pursue this vision of a perfect world is that humanity's life will perish without them.

"The idea of an American perfect world a more perfect union states of the US constitution a system approaching near to perfection," announces Benjamin Franklin. Though the idea of perfectibility of America was one of its own creation, we just put it in more simpler terms to help make it easier to understand the realities we are faced with. It is real that heaven can only be reached after death; the reality is that the garden of Eden is not a myth. When Thomas More wrote in his utopia in 1516, he named it no place.

On the contrary, the Americans created a more practical perfect world and established a national identity around it. America sets itself apart from citizens of other countries who bear commonalities in ethnicity, race, or religion. American citizens have distinctive features that distinguish us from one another; we do not have the same skin color nor do we speak the same language nor do we pray to the same God, but until recently, at least from sea to shining sea, we have shared one rarified presumption that within their borders, the best of what is will closely resemble the best of us.

Schemas for the vision for America is a continued effort to create that utopia, that perfect world. Without vision, it is impossible for man to realize a perfect society. Visions help man to build schemas of what he wishes to create and to build a mental model of aspects of the world.

A clear vision, a piece of literary work, opens windows into the light to what America's issues are today. How wisdom, logic, and common sense are utilized to provide reasoned resolutions to bring back our republic's exceptionalism which can serve to propel our country toward newfound prosperity. Referencing our republic's greatest threats and how to deal with them can help solve our problems. As Thomas Jefferson's "call to action" roll out revolutions, to name a few, it provides for a safe and secure country liberated from war and terrorism, small and limited streamlined government, balanced budgets free of deficits, and crushing the national debt and a fair and just simplified tax system that's free of bureaucracy. Also, there are vast economic opportunity with high-paying jobs for all and forward-looking practical immigration solutions. This is a mindset that brings all together with a common purpose and finally, a prosperity parallel to that of which our forefathers saw for our children.

"Where there is no vision the people will perish" is a proverb very apropos to a new Congress coming into session. The past should be our teacher to help us understand our past president and then lead us to the future.

The chairman of science and technology committee is expressly concerned that Congress needs to address the need for funding innovations and technology programs. To achieve the innovations of tomorrow, we must do a better job of educating our children including preparing students for advanced degrees and to make sure some of our young adults acquire mathematics literacy as a foundation for technology-based economy.

Notably, the country is continually confronted with a fiscal crisis. STEM education is a necessary investment that will encourage economic growth and assure Americans' future prosperity and success. The vision for America is a continued search for that perfect world. Without vision, it is impossible to create that perfect world.

> A vision for America is an idea for all citizens to take part in, to have a voice in our collective decisions, to establish real democracy. Never mind we do not need political parties to divide us any longer period ideas must overcome ideology. It is time for citizens to take responsibility for our future and become involved in our nation's destiny. When we work together anything is possible. (2020 vision for America)

A Vision for America: Shown by God to His Prophet Jonah

A message to the people of the United States of America given to me Jonah ben Noah, the prophet of animals, the book of Amos in the Bible.

> Shall a trumpet be blown in the city, and the people not be afraid? Shall there be evil in the city, and the Lord hath not done it? Surely the Lord God will do nothing, but he revealeth his secret unto his servants the prophets. The lion hath roared, who will not fear? the Lord God hath spoken. who can but prophesy? (Amos 3:6–8 KJV)

Jonah Ben Noah introduced himself to the people of the nation named by God. Jonah was to bring to the people a message that God has given to him for your nation. He asked the people to listen and take it honestly. There were several messages shown through visions. On May 10, 1985, Jonah, on top of a mountain on a beautiful day under clear skies, saw a cloud take on a form of an eagle soaring across the sky with wings spread and talon forward; the right wing disappeared which caused the head to push and be crushed in and disappeared, then the left wing was torn loose, and the body twisted out of shape.

On the thirteenth of May 1985, as I, Jonah Ben Noah, was sitting in the house at my table, the voice of the Lord God began to speak to me and give me the interpretation. He said unto me, *The eagle that you saw torn apart is America who has its wings of freedom taken away and its mind of life, liberty, and happiness crushed and vanished; the body that remains is so twisted and out of shape that it is no longer recognizable for what it was.*

God, in each message, reveals his displeasure with the people of America and what they were doing. One that he was especially displeased with was the way that Americans are not allowed to pray in school when he had demanded them to pray. God called us out for our many sins.

Noah was a prophet; he was the messenger. The words that Noah spoke were those of God. This is the word of God given to me to warn the people to return to his Word and live in the right way, for God loves righteousness.

George Washington, the father of our country, was a man of prayer and prophesized about America. He would go into the thicket many times during his time at Valley Forge to pray. He had many visions of angels appearing to him with the message. "As I continued looking, I saw a bright Angel on whose brow rested a Crown of light, on which was traced the word union he was bearing the American flag between a divided nation that said remember you are brethren."

An Honest Discourse: Utopia

The question is how can we build utopia when we have so many skeptics who believe it is impossible. These overshadowing remarks tend to shatter what could be of support for solving our world's crisis today. There are those who criticize utopian thinking and label it as socialism. We could solve the crisis we are at now as traditional solutions as of now have not worked. Lest we forget, utopia has shaped our nation; it has influenced our thinking toward humankind.

We have other renowned people who see utopia as hope for a better way of living. Hope and vision have a way of energizing people and making them more creative. The fighting for and against a utopian nation by different factions as the right versus the left and then there is the libertarians asserting their opinions of what a better world would look like. This only serves to keep the country torn apart and limits our progress.

Utopian hope has been researched and found to be social Utopians who have ambitions for creating a world of optimism by unleashing the best of human nature. In my opinion, what is unreal about hope not being a reality? What is unreal about wanting to live in a better world? Whether it helps or not help, it is worth holding on to. Like vision, without hope, people will perish, so it is worth our attention.

Utopia is *not* a new idea; it is an ideal revisited because of man's sinful ways and disobedience to God's Word. We have gone the gamut in search of ways to reconstitute the country to establish a government that recognizes all people. Utopia has brought a fair amount of fraught in our country. The literary works on utopia has attracted more factions or entities that can become confusing to one's acceptance of a utopian society.

There is no doubt that these theories are born out of discontent of this present-day world. So now, where do we go if the people go beyond these intellectual scientists and some of their research? We hearken back to the Bible which in Corinthians 13:13 says faith, hope, and charity. I say dwell on these things. While our intellectual institutions are extremely important on all levels and in all areas of our country, the Bible is our foundation, for which every living creature's existence on this earth depends.

I am pleased to read Rousseau's discourse. I am familiar with Rousseau as a philosopher and how he wrote prolifically on education and his thoughts on utopia and his visions for utopia.

What society looks like is repeated twice what one believes a perfect society looks like. Most invariably, they view a perfect society as one where things are always in harmony, no ills or health risks and no wars of any kind to plague society. In Rousseau's theory on society, he starts out talking about utopia, but over time, he moves further and further away from equality. If you were to read Rousseau's discourse, you would be apt to believe that Rousseau believed an ideal state of nature would be more desirous for people to live in.

But Rousseau's outlook to achieve a utopian society is a positive one. His feelings about utopia was expressed in his works and he writes, "I wanted to be born in a country when sovereign and the people could have bought one and the same interest. So that all the movements of the machine always tended common happiness." Rousseau says when everyone is working together for a common cause, there will be no opposition and no rebellion.

Rousseau has thoughts on government as well; he does not believe in having more than one political party. He thinks when there is more than one political party, it opens the door for disagreement, and that can lead to no greater good. Rousseau states, "In the state of nature, where everything takes place in such a uniform manner and where the face of the earth is not subject of those sudden and continual changes caused by the passing of people living together." He believes in a state of nature where everyone is harmonized because in this way, the general will can only be benefited.

In *The Concept of Utopia*, Ruth Levitias says, "Utopia expresses an explores what is desired under certain conditions; It also contains the hope that these desires may be met in reality rather than merely in fantasy. That the essential elements in utopia is not hope but in the desire the desire for a better way of living." Levitis is the author of a book to defend her definition of desire for utopia as opposed to hope. Both these terms can be functional in the discourse on utopia, but they both are seen as abstract but are concrete in terms that we use in discussing utopia.

There is a discourse on utopia from a philosophical view from our most knowledgeable savants who have a penchant for engaging in disputes over various topics such as moral philosophy. These men rarely enter into any psychological discourse without bringing up religion as a consideration. They feel that man's immortality makes him vulnerable to punishment in hell for his sinful ways, and heaven is his reward if he does what God demands. They use such terms as virtuous living by the laws of nature. They use reason as a pathway toward a goal of conformity. The great minds are more interested in nature. Lastly, reason tells us that we work toward happiness for all people to seek pleasure as a goal of life, but it can also limit us for that purpose.

> A map of the world that does not include utopia
> is not worth glancing at, for it leaves out the one
> country at which humanity is always landing.
> And when humanity lands there it looks out and
> sees a better country, sets sail, progress is the real-
> ization of utopia.

Bertoll Oman, a professor of politics, looked into this claim since this riveting nature left him unsettled. To him, Utopian at the beginning was nebulous as it relates to the ambiguous way of defining what it is. Moreover, his earlier writing explains utopia as being no place but some place. No place because it was described as being a perfect place which doesn't exist but a place that can be depending upon the people and society if it can be improved and has some notion of what it would look like.

To go back and forth in our discussion of whether utopia is possible or impossible does not show where we arrived at in these conclusions; is there a certain criteria one that can be proved or is valid? Probably not, since there is so such confusion in utopian thinking.

Confusion can come about when there is speculation on utopia whether utopia is realizable. To dream of utopia is a natural mental activity but to fantasize it is not the thing we should engage in and let go unchecked. It is one thing to build sandcastles and another to try to live in one.

This discussion is Marxist's opinion and of a utopian vision for the future, mostly of psychological and philosophical underpinnings.

Do logicians, psychologists, and eticists all attempt to define happiness? Some say happiness is living true to your core principles of your nature of being a virtuous person and applied to others; reasoning helps us keep to one's principles. It helps us make rational decisions about our life.

Ethicists would say virtue is equality in itself; virtue is a facet of justice, and that is what we seek for in today's society. The word *equality* has been repeated so often and is grounded in the Declaration of Independence that it is losing strength. Its profoundness has become just a filler in a sentence with no substance.

Becoming a utopian society means a society that recognizes all of its citizens as equals of self-worth. So there is no level of equality; it does not exist in steps. The word *equality* is not honored in a way that it is meant to be. Many of our citizens do not have complete equality as Black and Brown people are treated as second-class citizens. Socially, some states have made some strides in closing that gap, but there still remains a tinge of prejudice and discrimination and stereotyping.

America can't claim to be a utopian society as long as it continues to dismiss the most valuable document the Declaration of Independence composed by the founding fathers to send a message to the world that all men are created equal. It's a statement that seems conflicting during slavery and remains so today. The stain of racism is seemingly forever as much has happened to the Native Americans.

The original settlers bullied the Native Americans and through every treaty took land from them saying they were not humans just merciless savages. Equality has been lent out to other races than white in bits and pieces including equal job opportunities and equal education opportunities.

When one views the halls of Congress, you can see only white men making decisions based on antiquated laws that are centuries old, and only the elite are able to attend elite schools as in Ivy League colleges.

The Black and Brown students have difficulties in trying to be accepted in these institutions. But not because their SAT scores were too low, it may be because Black young men or ladies have to work after school to help their single mothers feed their siblings that they have at home; students from affluent families have parents that resort to cheating by paying for their children's scores to secure their child a spot in the very best schools. These types of activities have a domino effect on those who were denied a good education. This affects the individual's quality of life and perpetuates more inequality.

There is no equality when inequality exist based on religion, gender, and color. All people should have the same basic rights, the right of life, liberty, and the pursuit of happiness; equal rights are not enough without equal results. Income inequality and equal education are not enough on many fronts. Inequality exists because there is not equal education, and the dominant ones get the job. This explains why the innovation and major achievements that America's great bear the face of the white man.

A Revival of a New Society

A utopian society suggests equality for all, and all that is needed for this to materialize is to develop a more civilized society—one that addresses the needs of the people with an emphasis on a more humanitarian society. This is as simple as kindergarten: be kind; no hitting; no biting, sharing, and caring; all we need to know we learn in kindergarten.

Of course, no one nor anything is perfect, and society will never be perfect either. There are some who think government will never be perfect. Why not? Maybe this is because it is listening to many voices. Or well-founded government that adheres to the constitution looks to the constitution as a paradigm; we, as a country, let too many things divide us. We are more alike than we are different; this can easily be seen in a Venn diagram if we were to illustrate differences in our country.

Let us remove the word *perfect* when relating to our great nation because we know that there is no such thing as perfect. But we can surely make a better society. We can begin as imperfect and build toward improving upon it.

A society will not ever be perfect if its citizens think selfishly instead of realistically. The goal to create a perfect society means to fulfill everyone's happiness, not just your own. But then there are those who work for a social group to fulfill their happiness to the maximum at the expense of others.

Moreover, hypothetically speaking, if such a society did exist where each member agrees to commit to making everyone around him happy and no member resorts to hoarding happiness, can you imagine what kind of society that would be?

For example, we would be free of wars because war creates unhappiness. In order to create this perfect society that we speak of, we will have to first find ways to manage these problems and how to implement them.

> Caring for a person is the most potent ingredient for creating a perfect nation. Caring for the more able, the less able, serving each other is the rock upon which a good society is built. (Robert Greenleaf)

Simple things such as gifts and talent according to unique capabilities and resources and the reciprocity of all things. Any community who allows unemployed members to remain within its walls eventually perish because of them.

All over the world, it is evident that people have a great urgency for a better society and are working toward making it materialize. In order to create a better nation, we need to change our values. According to Jim Wallis, "We in the West, need rescuing from our moral an economics. These are underwater and need recovery from it if we are to ameliorate our society." The moral test for how healthy a society can be is predicated on the treatment of the most vulnerable in that society.

Our task for the development of leadership is to fortify the core values of ethical behavior according to God's assignment to us as servants; when these values become the basis for spiritual practices that live out within a specific community, over time, they gradually change.

> Modest doubt is called the beacon of the wise.
> (William Shakespeare)

When President Lyndon B. Johnson took the presidency, his main focus was on building a better society for the American people. His Great Society was to eradicate poverty; he wanted to expand government and secure economic opportunity and civil rights for all. President Johnson's vision for America was to improve life for the people better than what was offered to them at the time. A world in which the words *liberty and justice for all* had a real meaning.

President Johnson realized that the lack of education was the cause of poverty and other social problems, so he created many programs to address these problems. President Johnson took office in 1964 at a time when racial injustices were at a peak and many more inequalities that deterred the growth of a better society. Everyone should be a participant in society and nation building according to the president.

His education program began with the very young realizing that the early years of education are very important. He created the head start program, especially focusing on towns along the Appalachians where there was abject poverty. To ensure more equitable opportunities for all, he also had a sweeping consumer protection policy.

The president's wife, First Lady Bird Johnson, adopted a beautification project aimed at cleaning up and beautifying the highways. When President Johnson expressed his desires for a better society, who would have thought that this was indeed utopian thinking.

> Keeping people poor is a political choice we can no longer afford; With so much potential wasted we need a universal basic income. (Rutgers Bregman)

Margaret Thatcher once called poverty a personality defect; though, to many, it is a bridge too far. It is inconceivable for one to perceive that there is something wrong with people. The conception of the poor has been a commonly held belief by many for a long time until it was suddenly realized that this was an erroneous belief.

Poverty and what causes poverty has been a topic of study for many psychologists; their studies include from all over the world aimed at farmers. They are using farmers as their subject before harvest time, and after harvest time, and its effects of their work and salary. Farmers are paid one lump sum annually. This essentially means he is financially able only one part of the year; the other part, he is unable. Psychologists conducted experiments testing the farmer's IQ suggesting that their intelligence was such that they were unable to make intelligent decisions about their lives. They did not state the variables that may or may not have played a part of the outcome of this test. As it turns out, according to some, it is a scarcity, not mentality. It is notable that people behave different when they perceive things are scarce. In their attempt to analyze poor people, they overlook the humanitarian side and the soul of these people, but they do acknowledge and conclude that a universal basic income is needed. It is not an opinion, not a favor but a right.

America: An Idea or a Country

Is America an idea, country, or both? America is viewed by some as being both an idea and a country. It is described as unique and is an attraction to people all over the world; people don't just dream of coming to America but look to assimilate in this new world. America continues to open its doors to people of all creeds and race and ethnicity; many of these people are escaping persecution and seeking religious freedom that were not afforded to them in their native countries.

The question that is asked, why is the United States a global superpower? There are many responses to this question, all of which have played an important part of the answer; among some of these is our geographic fortune to be surrounded by oceans and neighbors who are friendly—an enormous expanse of land with vast resources. A Democratic system of government leadership is wise and stable and are exceedingly accomplished citizens and a military second to none. These are just some of the reasons why America has been predominant for all of the twentieth century and when America rose to be the only superpower during the Cold War and has remained unchallenged in our ability to project influence across the globe.

During the nineteenth and twentieth century, there were many immigrants coming to America; they were not doing a cost benefit analysis to distinguish between the struggles of the military and the landmass of other European countries. The enormous amount of people came to America from around the globe because they liked many of the things that America stood for, especially our democratic system of government stated in the first three articles of the constitution.

What is not what it is, is when people globally and historically viewed the United States not just as a place on a map but something bigger. They admired the geographical features, the vast oceans, and the iconography of Emma Lazarus's Statue of Liberty welcoming all to its shores. Send these the homeless tempest to me; I lift my lamp toward the golden door. The icons have meaning. The icons to them have value far beyond; these words give a feeling of expression of patriotism. They feel that these icons offer hope and give them something to strive for. Their hope is for a better life one that offers safety and prosperity as well as equality and justice for all.

America is indeed an idea that is unique in many ways and is the reason people worldwide seek to come here. People not only dream of coming to America; they have hopes of becoming American. For years, men and women traveled through rough conditions which, in many instances, could have cost them their lives to reach the American shores. These immigrants escaped the Soviet Union, communist China, and other countries hoping to find some refuge from oppression.

When it comes to America, the everyday American exhibits naivete of the two facts about America. The first fact is when the two parties Democrats and Republicans speak of America, they envision something different than what everyday Americans do; the second caveat is that Republicans and Democrats in government and big media relationships can convey a false appearance of disagreement. Quite the contrary, they are of agreement; they are together in their conception of America, period. From this point, all things cleared up and void of any ambiguities. American ideas are the first and only nation in all human history to have been founded upon principle and proposition.

There are so many features that identify America other than geographic. The military might be the most salient as it crosses cultural and transhistorical. America is unique in its duplicity in that it claims to be justice-led to the purpose of political and economic borders.

In the Rotations
of the Universe periodically,
the Destiny Dial clicks
to that space
called Community.
Then all the world
celebrates
and weeps—
tears
which sparkle
and reflect
each hope,
each dream;
when we all plant
our Heart Flower Seeds
in the garden
hoping for the Future
which heals.
Not Miracles
but Peace,
not Riches;
but Shared Prosperity;
not no fear
but lessened anxiety.
America is an Ideal.
Every once in a while
She produces that hand
which re-lights the torch
of Lady Liberty
near extinguished by extremity;
a new hand which reaches out
to millions of other hands
which reach back

affirming the simple
retort:
Yes We Can.
Sing now
as others have sung
for phase, line and meter
bring back the music,
only America can sing,
of an era
which maybe,
just maybe
will crack that shut door,
where Hope's light will
shine through
upon child faces
where the children glimpse
new possibilities;
where new shinings
illuminate each child-face
bless each
and their progeny;
all bathed now in that precious prospect
where there is respect
for lives human and non-human.
Where peace is not extinguished
by flesh-mauling war machines.
American is an idea
that won't die;
an experiment
amid swarms of tyrannies;
where sometimes
the Universal Clock Pointer
swings round
to that wondrous space
we call
Liberty;

and Peace;
All this
signaled potentially
by a goat herder's son
who had that same dream.
Democracy is that system
best preserved
because no one knows
where Potential
emanates from;
or lessons that can be learned
from a goats herders son
and that Kansas wife
who had a different dream.
(Lonnie Hicks)

How would a government look in a utopian world? Moon, a counselor and psychologist, describes a true utopian government as mostly individual, self-motivated, and a utopian government is not necessary in a utopian world. Everyone would think highly of themselves to not respect others, so respect is reciprocal in a utopian world. They care for each other and themselves and all the creatures of the world, human and animals; everyone would cooperate to do their part.

The people would show their gratitude with overwhelming exuberance. They would value fair exchange and would be well-versed in teamwork eager to fill in whenever necessary without hesitation and for whatever reason or cause. They would hail acceptance and equality but regret war, crime, and hatred. There would be no need for judges because there would be no need for judging. Deb Moon doubts that kind of government could exist in today's society in the United States.

I say if genetics can affect one's thinking and decision-making, maybe our genetics can come up with a formula that can create such a society. We do need to create a better world; historically, utopian governments were one of the first that the early settlers decided right after they adopted their new home. It was made up of some of the old government that the settlers thought was proven to be successful with new utopian ideas. A monarchy was decided upon first to give utopia a sense of unity but including some elements of democracy such as the ability to impeach the ruler. They did not want to give too much power to one person to prevent any one person from becoming too powerful. This approach was archaic compared to the present time except for the impeachment being a part of the new government as well as the old.

All of society is under some type of government control. Everyone adheres to the rules of government. Government is not inherently bad; well-educated people are needed to regulate society. Sadly, we have all kinds of government; some are good, and some are bad. a Democratic government is designed to work for everyone, but unfortunately, many of our governments do not work this way. More often, they put themselves first before the citizens, and they make deals with multinational companies under the guise of helping to improve the economy which has proven to be untrue.

The prerequisites to a utopian government sound similar to our current constitution:

1. The constitution would have a bill of rights that would enumerate all the rights of people. Life, liberty, and the pursuit of happiness would be listed.
2. The constitution would specify that the only right of government is to protect the right of every citizen.
3. The representatives would be selected randomly from a pool of literate and educated people thus guaranteeing that every profession, race, color is proportionally represented.
4. The judicial system would not punish. The judicial system would have fair restitution; minimal prophylaxis would be used, one necessary to minimize harm to citizens.
5. The majority of the people or representatives could not vote to spend money on anything that did not benefit equality.

Metaphorically, our government is America's lung, and it is on fire. We do not need a rocket scientist to tell us that. It is, however, something to ponder about how we got to where we are and how do we fix it.

The word *dystopia* is described as the opposite of utopia. Dystopia means a place where everything has gone wrong; authors write to express their concerns about society and humanity and to tell the people as members of the society to be alert to what is happening in society in which they live. Be careful, especially in your society's "shock and awe," and be observant of the changes that can take place.

Jean Card writes, "Big government and big media are dominating American Society and suffocating free speech, who will rise up?" According to Card, America is beginning to look more like chapters that precede futuristic fiction, dystopian fiction to be exact. Aside from the shock and awe of the presidential election, there is continuous jihadist threats globally, the specter of Armageddon, global warming, and the widespread dysfunction of economy. The cultural tectonic plates around the world are disrupting people's lives as we speak.

Dystopian society is more of a reality than we realize. Much of what the Lupien novelist has written can be observed in the United States today. Small businesses are nonexistent; only corporations that are working alongside big government are seen.

To this point, Jean Card writes on dystopia and big government how the two are dominating America's society and is suffocating free speech and wonders who will rise? Who will speak up to save America? Card, in her opinion, states,

> America is beginning to resemble a page out of futuristic fiction expressing "shock and awe" of the president's election; what with ongoing of the jihadists of an epic proportions of Armageddon, global warming [climate change]. On the economy exponentially dysfunctional. The culture change in politics that are taking place and seems to be reaching a crescendo—and the many cul-

tures around the world are forming a "tectonic plates"—upsetting people lives and is present as we speak.

Card is painting a picture of a dystopian society that we all should be concerned about and wonder if it is becoming more real; are we at a prequel here in America today?

Small businesses are practically all gone away; only corporations are working with big government. Technology is unrecognizable because of its advancement that, say, happened so fast that it is almost "magical."

The source of our information is centralized. The oppressed have to fight for things that are supposed to be rightfully theirs as afforded them through the constitution. Our current government is dysfunctional—a charismatic doctrinaire, president, has mainly caused a delay in the progress of our country; stalemate is the new norm. It seems *pros and cons* lead the charge in polarizing and paralyzation.

PART II

PART II

Is the American Dream Dead, Deferred, or Delayed?

> Just because the American dream existed
> for generations of Americans doesn't
> mean we can put on our blinders.
> —Branden King

Has the American dream died during the great recession that effected the economic system caused an economic downfall, or is it just in recess waiting for those who work hard enough to breathe life into it? The stock markets have ensued most of our dollars (Statistics reports, Paradis, 2009). These losses, along with unemployment, for the past years have played a role in this creation of the dismal prospect in the U.S, but it is believed that Americans, America's values, and ideals are still alive.

The American dream has caught the attention of many, and some have written about it; we, as citizens in these United States, have always had a dream of a better life for all. We have hopes that life would be richer with opportunity for each of them where hard work is valued and equal pay for equal time; there is respect for all according to one's ability to achieve regardless of one's religious leaning, political affiliation, and ethnicity. The dream is for a safe place where honesty and integrity is honored and the opportunity to live a safe and secure way of life.

America today has taken on a different face; we have become a more divided country. For some, the dream is dead. Others who are valued think that is still very much alive. It is imperative for overcoming the residuals of the Great Recession and overcome poverty; bring the dream to light.

Historians define the "American Dream" as perfect; this leads us to believe that the world is a perfect place. But the fact is that there is no perfect place, of course not; sometimes, I feel that it is more dystopian.

There is something about America in spite of the dream that seems to be moving further away; people from all over the world come here to share a dream.

The Declaration of Independence made a promise dating back 1776 which is the original dream. In recent years, it has been noticeably clear that there is a hiatus between the original promise (dream) and the new one that exists now. The nation is more exclusive; prosperity is enjoyed by some people but not so much for others. The original dream had three strands: the first is prosperity; the second and third are democracy and freedom for all, originally, but this was soon looked down upon, ergo, a dystopian though and has been since then a nation of mistrust—a dystopian society.

The American Promise
and the America

Dream are the two hopes—one that people hold dear and thought they could count on you; this is why they traveled to this country for...

In 1776, the promise to the American people was equal citizenship, human liberty, and a government for the people, by the people, and has strove to fulfill it.

The American promise was so sincere that Lyndon B. Johnson, during his presidency, was fighting for Blacks, in this case, for voting rights.

President Johnson called upon the nation to fulfill its covenant with God and man, and President Johnson authored in his speech, "We shall overcome" and thus the promise was sealed. The actual title of his speech was The American Promise.

It may be a "stretch" of the imagination to believe that nations can live among each other in peace, equality, and unity; can we say that utopia will not be achievable in a real sense of the word? And does the notion that nations among and between in peace, equity, and justice seem too ideal to be true? According to the skeptics, this is a common and healthy thought. However, the idea of attempting a perfect, more better society should never be dismissed for "every attempt to make a great change in existing conditions—every lofty vision of possibilities for the human race has been labeled, Utopia" (Emma Goldman).

By comparison to the other modernistic world, in the United States' Utopia, we have the privilege of free speech while this is not true in other nations, and we have a constitution; we have the privilege to travel at our disposal around the world—go to other countries and broaden our horizon—and observe nature at its best, "God's handiwork." We are always in agreement in some things, and for the most part, we are always willing to come to the aid of those who are in need of us, to compromise in any differences that we may have even in the case of other countries; America is not perfect, but compared to the rest of the world, it is Utopia. This is the opinion of some.

In today's society, in the United States, dystopia society is recognized through biases and information that is oftentimes misleading to influence the American people to succumb to some ideologue engaged to control a society perpetually overlooking the people; "The big eye" leave people with little trust of the outside world. Some ways a dystopian society is viewed is through fiction, profound politics, governing class as told by H.G. Wells, *The Sleeper Awakes*. Many people see our governing class as more or less "dictatorial Congress" as in the example of the parable of the sower in Matthew 13:1–23; it would require heaven to see the truth that the kingdom is slowly progressing, and if that be so, people don't express confidence in it anymore and strongly disapprove of the president—that is revealed in the way NSA treated Snowden in spite of the fact that he was looked upon as a threat to the country.

The sayings "this or that" or some happenings are stranger than fiction (at least is the way that it is viewed by futurist writers to allude to the concept). Moreover, some of writings by the futuristic writers seem to be true...they always seem to be able to get it right as it relates to the country's direction. For example, the futuristic writers explained the economic system through *Rollerball*. *Rollerball*, frightening as it may seem, they could foresee that the economy is under control of corporation and face elements from the *Rollerball*.

The human masses voice their concern of being lowly and degrading, and smaller groups who had the opportunity to acquire an education were only afforded the "elite."

Also, dystopian fiction, many times, juxtaposes the "upper and lower" classes or incorporating privation and corporatism when large corporation that were owned privately have efficaciously took over government, as it relates to policies making and decision-making.

They manipulate, infiltrate, control, and bribe or contracted by or otherwise function as a government.

According to Harrison Bergman, our ability to accomplish are being constrained by having to comply to egalitarian likening to social norms of inequality as in *Fahrenheit 451*—the social society that cater to the intellectuals with a particular force (passion); violence is seen in various dystopians delineated in war and criminal acts while in 1984 delineated environment, air quality for human and plants.

Real or imagined, dystopia is becoming real; every day, the futurist and writers of fiction have breathed life into them as they prove that fiction is not strange. Dystopia, as a society, is the opposite of a utopian society that is mirroring a futuristic society while considered as fiction.

Along with a "shock and awe" of the presidential election, we are constantly in conflict with terrorist, jihadist expansion, global warming, and an economically financial dysfunction as the language of politics are creating layers of culture that are continuing.

Where are we headed, and who will turn things around? Are we headed backwards, 1984, Huxley's *Brave New World* or Fritz Lang *Metropolis?* The current government's branches are dysfunctional; we have a legislature that is extremely partisan and a president who has a penchant for coercing citizens or use the *Art of Persuasion* to go along with political ideologies and has had caused a veritable mountain of stress-rendering polarization. A Supreme Court made up of elites break the long stalemates at least until they themselves become a stalemate on the rebels (limited government, conservatives).

It is evident that America today is much like science fiction described in another world at another time; small business is a thing of the past. Aside from the usual behemoths, big government, economic woes, and struggle for basic rights, we could say "we've overcome."

Utopia Is Dystopia

In George Orwell's novel *Animal Farm*, there is a futuristic dystopia society that is ruled by a communist party and a man named "Big Brother." "One of the main concepts of dystopia is that it hides things from people and assumes the status of perfection because nobody sees the flaws if the people see the flaws that lacks in their government the government will fail" (David Durett).

There are no two people who give the meaning of Utopia in the same way, and here's where the problem is born.

To some people, a place where no one has to work would not sound right to people who needed to work for a living and have worked all their adult lives, and work is "life." Being productive and a contributor to productivity doesn't find this to be a good citizen, it would be dull and, quite frankly, boring.

Vegan is a choice for those who loves animals and does not want to come to this; however, for those who like eating meat during the meal, to put it clearly, a carnivore Utopia is when animals innocently and contently (cows) gave their lives to be eaten and that would hurt vegans.

Unlike Utopia that wishes to make everyone happy and pleased, in dystopia, this is the problem and the reason why it is sad; Utopia creates dystopia, yet it is worth striving for. One person's Utopia could be another person's dystopia, and it can go the other way around.

This contributed to the uniqueness of the human diversity in desires and differences of culture crucial, and it would not be ethical to pose your Utopia on others.

What makes society a Utopia? Utopia is by definition contains highly desirable qualities nearly perfect in nature; it depends on the person that you are, and it is individual and personal.

One man's Utopia can be another person's dystopia; the reason given, we all don't live in Utopia. We have no idea what a utopia looks like, so therefore, we can't share the same idea; to go a bit further, a misogynist would not likely share a feminist view of utopia. And so it is with Utopia; most people perceives as a Supreme Society two political parties collaboratively engaged in a debate on what they deem a utopia should be like and how to construct one and how to implement one. When they concluded, some could see their Utopia in the environment and "humanitarian" in nature with a focus on the poor who timidly try to work hard to keep up with their "peers" while all working together harmoniously.

Utopia, in itself, doesn't have what is required to sustain a society and would instantly turn into a dystopia; to be a society that is perfect as Utopia, it would necessitate a suppression of those things of human qualities—those traits that make humans human biologically. And because many humans, by nature, are competitive and have the prosperity to survive and have a group mentality, in this sense, "a society where there is an imbalance of power struggle is labeled." In group community, it is to be apart or is a society that cannot be sustained. Utopia would find these sources of inequities and divisiveness but use an increased oppression (dystopia) methods to enforce the system.

My Utopia—Your Utopia: A Little or the Light Side

This story is an expression of one person's explaining her Utopia—what her Utopia would look like having spent hours pleading with her brains to come up with an idea for the world that would be best. When I was creating, I got an epiphany came out from nowhere. My Utopia may be your dystopia. I could create my utopia with anything that I desire. A complete antheses from your desires, then it becomes someone else's dystopia; another thought that entered my mind while creating my utopia is what is the actual meaning of the word? It originated from the Latin word, meaning "no place"—citing a reason for this that no one has come up with a way to create Utopia that does not gradually changes over time into dystopia; the translation for dystopia is bad, poor place; the reasoning being the opposite of Utopia is "poor and corrupt" which is dystopia. This is a sudden thought like light bulbs going off and on. I asked the question, What can cause "my utopia" to transform into dystopia, and better yet, how could my rules and laws transform into Utopia? What was in my rules and laws that control and change my utopia completely.

In my Utopia, there are laws; law numbers have been established. Law number 27 states about honesty: the leader has to be honest and make decisions based on reasonable sense that everyone can follow; to the average person, this sounds like a splendid idea, but wait, what if the leader comes into power and establishes a law that would exclude people of certain races and you think this to be unacceptable, and this is iniquitous. However, the leader uses propaganda techniques and wise speeches to influence every one—that he is the leader and his laws are to make things better; right away, we have lost "equality" because the people are considered in a lower status which shows everyone that the leader status has just been upgraded. Instantly, my utopia is no longer diverse; this would be complete inequality due to the fact that I no longer have that race (people), and those people feel unwanted and become stuck in a dystopia. To extend this thought, what if the leader made a law to hate all these cultures and not the leader; your reward is your freedom to express your independence. All cultures could be adversely affected by the manipulation of propaganda in a way that all cultures and diversity would be eliminated, thus total inequality. In addition to that, people who were working "independent thought" were in the process of losing it because that had been manipulated and became under complete control of the leader. Law number——, "No one is allowed to destroy, demolish, judge, or choose to be negative and racist toward someone's religion." This law was made predicated on my belief that diversity is a crucial part in any society, so I, the writer, felt compelled to include this in my utopian laws, but what if this law exceeds in its intent? Obedience to this law is clear, which could have a direct effect on other people disobeying this law. This in turn creates a cycle of evil and the loss of "utopian aspects and characteristics," and here again is another way to make what was perfect transition to "oppressive and corrupt," transformed from utopia to a dystopia state.

Here's another chilling thought: let's say the leader decides to keep these cultures totally equal; it would be necessary to have equal amount of people in the culture in case there are too many people who were linked to a particular culture. The governments least favored from that group would be eradicated by some means; this is clearly dystopia.

Perhaps we have shown you the power of dystopia in action. It was a desire to know (the writer) how equal law could gradually form layers of red, and how each law rules transition into intense regulations and controls. My, writer, law number 1—everyone votes for a leader; this is more sane. Also, it is more aligned with democratic philosophy.

Of course, there are ways that this could go wrong. They could vote for a person who denies the laws—a sinister person; this person, with no help from anyone, can alone wreck the country and break any peace or perfectness and thereby destroy the society.

Law 4, the leader's term in office is four years, and law 4 also establishes the terms after law 4, the times in office; the leader is prohibited from voting for the next two elections. Law 5, it is not allowed to destroy the Utopia aspects of the world or make laws against diversity and culture. Law 6, racism is not allowed and banned completely. Law number 9 is banning an hierarchy and banning social hierarchy and people having a higher or lower socio-income status.

The last law which is law 10, is where everyone gets the same amount of money for the same amount of time working because job equality is important to society. The writer did not establish laws number 7 and 8, why?

It is clear that the writer's attempt to prove that there is potential for dystopia in every Utopia eloquently and hypothetically written in her story as the reader can see in each writer's Utopian law that there is a dystopia overtones (in the womb of the Utopia, a dystopia is waiting to be born).

This happens immediately when Utopia is defined as "no place." It is no place for reasons explained in the story and repeated in some other writings.

Better stated, in each Utopia, there are seeds of dystopia that can grow and supersede Utopia. When under poor leadership, there is no reason why we do not keep working toward creating a better world.

The ten laws, while hypothetical, provoke thoughts because these would be considered when thinking a society against a society (Utopian versus dystopian) to go into the human mind—how the human perceive Utopia and dystopia.

While this is hypothetically written by one who appears to be a student, it contains elements of profound thoughts and reasoning; it is unfortunate that it resembles the theory stating that for every action, there is an opposite and equal reaction.

Should America Strive for Utopia?

Utopia was "unearthed" by Thomas More back in the fifteenth century; it sometimes give the appearance of a place—a nonexistent place—because it is supposed to be a place of perfection. At times, it gives the appearance of a specimen—a creature that baffles philosophers, social scientists, and economists; they seem to be hard-pressed to deal with it because while they feel that it is more of an ideology and never come to be happy, it's a "zero" at the outset, so what can be done? You can't entertain this idea; the world would end up going backward.

In order to make this a more perfect world, we would have to consider some things that are real; for instance, the environment, physical, could be a deterrent to acquiring that perfect society. The environment, economy, and politics are issues that, more than not, align themselves with the needs of the people, not to mention the limitation of resources and not afforded freedom of travel for intellectual stimulation and psychological contentment.

Because things of this nature are not universal, some people might be affected by them while there are others who might experience the opposite affect; also, it does not tell the practical "limitations," and the "sustainability" is not there present where every member is doing what they please. Utopia is not likely to be achieved.

However, when we take a look around current society and its progress, it seems to be moving in a positive direction despite the disapproval, for the most part, of our government and politicians; the people in general seem to be content as the way things are.

Is This Striving for Utopia?

David Cameron—while primarily interested in reaching the moon, this is one step away from Mars—succinctly started that ideology is not what motivates politicians to seek Utopia; it is necessary to strive toward this "perfect world." It would be a detriment to society if we didn't; our society would regress. Human beings are inclined to be content and is always seeking for something different; as during our general election, the focus is on change, and they can see many things that could be changed.

Of course, the society does have many horrible problems in many instances, but more than that, people need change and progress in order to sustain the same level of happiness. If things don't change for a long time, we become anxious, unhappy, and all our contentment wanes and deteriorate, so to stay strong for Utopia, because it's twofold, strive for improvement; it is a requirement to the people in maintaining general happiness.

> The world we have created it is a process of our thinking. It cannot be changed without changing our thinking. (Albert Einstein)

Should America strive for Utopia? This question is answered by drawing on people from all echelon; some answered with a question of their own such as, Is a utopian society we should strive for, or is it financial freedom, health opportunity that's usually reserved for just a select few?" The idea of a utopia has become a concept and is described in many different ways. Can we really live in a perfect world without considering equality for all? From a vantage point, equality of the economy, education, politics, and society has been for a select few.

Also, in order to have a perfect society, people would have to be perfect, and what would one look like? Another thought on Utopia, adversely, Utopia seems to some as impossible; the structure of the economic system for example, if everyone is equal and would contend that technology has peaked to such an imaginary level, there will be no need for people to work, and as a result, a Utopia would be representative of people no longer progressing in any significant way. Everything is becoming as one, and Utopia will become dystopia in the eyes of people.

The reason why mankind has to strive for Utopia is to prove that it is achievable despite of some thinking differently. Nevertheless, it's about thinking in working toward—maybe not a perfect world—a better world. They want to be the ones who fix all that is broken in this world and who finds and bring more happiness in the world; after all, isn't it the "ups and downs" and the "in-betweens" of life that allow us to distinguish happiness and emotions?

The concept of Utopia from a perspective of internal healing is, How can this be, or how can this be achieved? Is it obtainable when we have to deal with the loss of a loved one and we became overshadowed by the thought of, *Could I have prevented it?* It is just…it is in these instances we look for new laws; one such law was named after a child's loss: Madison law or Charles law. Even though we know that, we wish to dismiss the idea; there is no fail-safe methods to stop these ugly things from happening in our effort to fix thing after thing. There are things that we have no control of, and then we hoped for Utopia for Utopians; it may have instead make it more difficult for others and ourselves, probably. This is one more reason why we strive to create Utopia.

The unenlightened with varied beliefs can learn to survive and live together to enlightened with no beliefs and objective reasoning can thrive in a Utopia.

Do our beliefs cloud our vision—a reason for Utopia to think clearly about Utopia? One of our visionaries think that to create a better world than what we live in now, he uses an analogy to make a point; a nonfunctional vehicle cannot function when it has many bad parts, so it is with our world, and it would be disingenuous to hope for when its occupants are not utopian. Therefore, the occupants is obligated to desire to become utopian (a.k.a. enlightened or clear thinking). Only when we use the power of reasoning that we are able to achieve enlightenment.

Sadly, however, your reason is not clear or the objective is constructed and prevented by our beliefs, values, and morals.

Holding out for the "right person," faith in a supreme being (deity), and some words of wisdom from a guru or some mundane things such as thinking that a woman's place is in the home, and money can't bring you happiness, these are typical, of course. Beliefs aren't necessarily "truths." They are void of any convictions or evidence; they hold firm, oftentimes, subconsciously. Reasoning follows our path (oftentimes subconsciously) that, in a subtle way, go around our beliefs to avoid causing a disturbance or unsettlement.

Because almost all beliefs are untruths, and there is no amount of reasoning, regardless of it being impenetrable, will yield a valid conclusion and understanding; ergo, the first that is needed is to *identify and eliminate* your beliefs.

Utopia can only be realized through your reasoning power, clear thinking. You cannot rely on your beliefs that are not "truths." Eliminate your beliefs; they only serve to thwart your reasoning by clouding your thinking.

America should continue in its effort to create more of a Utopia. Every man, woman, and child deserve to live in a better world, and it is incumbent upon the people to provide it for them.

There are two social stratification systems; one is vastly different from the other and is predicated on class.

If you look at a cut rock or a stratified rock, you will see layers of material, colors, density and thicknesses, and so it is with society; there are layers in the social stratification that are shown in the differences in freedom of opportunities, beliefs, color, and gender. These differences were to establish the level of society one can move within as well as how other members of society view you. The two social stratification systems, one is a closed system, and the other is an open social system. The dichotomization of the two systems will reveal a great contrast between the two. For example, if you are in the closed system, your freedom of movement is restricted, and you have no jurisdiction over the choices, and you are not able to change your status; you are of the lower status. On the other hand, by contrast, the open social stratification system can achieve and change status by virtue of working hard enough and searching hard; you can behave badly, and your status would not change.

So you may ask, What does this have to do with achieving a better world? Well, Utopia or to achieve a better world, equality is very important; social injustice is not liberal.

Social stratification goes beyond wealth; it spans into other entities and groups, organization, and metamorphs into a power and to an authoritarian right down the ranks. It is rather unnerving to think the power to the extent that they can assign status in schools, clubs, businesses, and, God forbid, my friend and my peers?

It is little comfort to realize whatever social stratification it takes, it can show up as having the ability to make rules, decisions, and put forth notions of "right and wrong."

Social stratification has serious negative impulse on society, and it is said to be the cause of inequality in economic, social, and political, "the big three." Aren't these three the backbone of the country? They serve to delineate people based on their wealth, power, and of their importance in society causing a social disparity and developing a virtual class system. Ergo, giving the people on the lower runs of the ladder an inferiority feeling; when this kind of disparity is allowed to happen, it causes chaos and thus get in the way of progress to creating a better world.

There is no society that all the people are all the same. People differ in their personal character; they are more heterogenous, except for one, and they are different in the social acceptance criteria and are socially differentiated. They are not treated as equal and could be denied social reward status, power, or income; simply put, the term *social inequality* refers to the existence of socially created inequality—dystopian.

Namaste

"I honor the place in you, in which the entire universe dwells. I honor the place in you that is light, love, truth, peace and wisdom. When you are in that place in that place in you, and I am in that place in me, we are one."

From the early existence of America, it has been a nation with "heart" and welcomed people from all over the world without minding their color, ethnicity, and race; my doors are open to you. Our founding fathers succinctly and eloquently penned the Constitution of the United States which promises you that you're endowed with certain alienable right. Among these are life, liberty, and the pursuit of happiness, and we make a covenant with God as stated in the Declaration of Independence.

Sadly, these laws and promises have been broken; the people do not have faith in government, and the government has served only to divide the country and its self-interest. In the patriotic song "America," "the purple mountain majesty, the purple majesty" has been viscerated by the two political parties: the red party and the blue party who are often in conflict will make it impossible for that purple mountain again. And the idea of "fruited plain" and low-hanging fruit which can likely be achieved, and it does not require a lot of effort, except if you are fortunate to have the opportunity to obtain an education adequately to achieve it.

Even immigrants who come to America, who came to the land of the free, are met with disappointment; they felt isolated, disenchanted. They can't use their talents and resources to engage in the political process or the social party or society and could incite protests.

Immigrants came to America to enjoy many of the opportunities that make life better for them, though there were those who were unsuccessful and were sorry that they came while those who were successful were glad that they did, which is a normal behavior.

America has been disappointing immigrants for a long time. For many immigrants, America is the *Golden Medina*, like no other, and a chance for their future to be better than what they left behind; they were confident of their chances to succeed, and that chance would be as equal as any other. They were expecting to sit at the table and share the meal; these are the things that are worth risking their lives for. Religious freedom was at the forefront. Immigrants don't understand until they get here and began to assimilate in the "New World" that America isn't as perfect and heavenly as they had imagined; there are limitations to their movement in getting to become American, thus they will be disappointed. They will find that America has been disappointing immigrants for a long time.

Benjamin Franklin in his infamous essay, "Those Who Remove to America"—an essay that was mainly to make Europeans aware that they have formed, through ignorance, mistaken ideas and expectations of what it is to be obtained there. Some were expecting high office, fortune, and respect.

Moreover, it served as precautionary measures to warn of separation between "expectations and reality" outlying all the hopes that gave impetus to people to come here in the beginning.

Here's a quote:

> Strangers are welcome because there is room enough for them all land therefore the old inhabitants are not jealous (distrustful) of them. Thus Laws protect them sufficiently so that they have no need of patronage of men—and everyone will enjoy security to profits of his industry.

Today how true these words are; immigrants are disappointed.

People of different cultures, races came America; it was soon a "melting pot." One America but sometimes, there are more conflicts that develop between them, mostly between the immigrants and minorities. America's rich history in education and other humanitarian excursions, unfortunately their idea was misconstrued; observing gross discrimination against minorities left the immigrants crestfallen, and the whites seem oblivious to this kind of behavior. They observed how the minorities were manipulated and had a poor chance for upward mobility.

Immigrants continued to be disappointed, marginalized, and treated so differently than one ever could imagine. America is a beacon of hope.

Hope is a thing with feathers like those of the American eagle that stands out as a reminder to all no matter the circumstances; each and every one of us has this entity within that always help us out by singing.

And to add to them disdain for America is told in this quote:

> I have not signed a Treaty with the United States Government—displays a story of resistance to the United States by declaring it "terminated; and demanding to go so far away we won't remember you ever been here." (11, 12, 26—The Indians express the same.)

America opens its arms to welcome immigrants to its shores, but upon entering in, they find the doors are closed or only just partially cracked on the dreams they had anticipated in the "nation" with so much promise; instead, they were met by so much deception. Educational is there but only to a certain population; jobs are available but only those no one else wants and mostly low-paying. Upon graduation, the alien, they are referred to now as the graduate who has to attach a green card on their diploma. Suppose if the student wants to return to their native country which could be anywhere around the world, then they would be competing with American companies, and not to mention, there is the possibility of being deported; walls will be built to curtail entrance into the country—overwhelmed with xenophobia, rhetoric, naturism, racism, and deprived of religious freedom.

Nativism began to creep its way into the minds of Americans. Americans began to resort to nativism when the country was going through some downfall and times when instability threatens national security, and there was a need to protect the natural-born against the immigrants. Benjamin Franklin warned—the word *warned* sound ominous, has nativism—immigrant groups in the United States with a little humor in cartoon style:

> In 1775—This sense of Nativism before America even gained independence—A colony of aliens who will shortly be so numerous as to Germanize us instead of anglifying them and will never adapt our Language or customs any more than can acquire our complexion, observations concerning the increase of mankind, peopling of countries, etc. 1755.

This sense of nativism today is mostly directed toward Mexican and Muslim immigrants and has crescendoed to an alarming pitch; politicians has circled their rhetoric as if it is "roadkill" picking a part/parts that benefit them, though some approach this nation with more civility in trying to find something to make policy reform.

> When the culture of deception continues to grow, it is important that followers of Christ must live in integrity and honesty. (Anon)

America is a pluralistic society, a melting pot and needs pluralistic thinking because of its magnitude. America is, at its very core, a nation of a diverse society; a pluralistic society has to have tolerance for his members of diversity of its different cultures to suppress any notion of stereotyping.

Be it melting or pluralistic society, there has been created by people from different countries—whom have come to America based on some perception of the United States—a promise made by the Constitution of the Declaration of Independence, and they have enriched our country economically, technologically, linguistically, and in science arbitrarily.

Einstein is one of many immigrants who came to America and has been a credit to our society.

To its end, this credit is given to some immigrants while we have Blacks, Muslims, and Mexicans who have been isolated. Stereotyping created such terms as xenophobic overtones and cries of nativism.

It may be a stretch of the imagination to believe that nations can live among each other in peace, equality, and unity, can they?

Some say that Utopia will never be achievable in the real sense of the word, and the notion that nations can live among and between in peace, equality, and justice seems too ideal to be true, according to the skeptics, which is common and healthy thought. However, the idea of attempting a (perfect) move to a better society should never be dismissed for "every attempt to make great change in existing conditions, every lofty vision of possibilities for the human race has been labeled Utopian" (Emma Goldman).

By comparison to the other modernistic world, the United States is Utopia; we have the privilege of free speech while this is not so true in other nations, and we have the constitution. Travel privileges are at our disposal to go to other countries to widen our horizons and observe nature at its best—God's handiwork. We are always in agreement in some things, but for the most part, we are always willing to come to the aid of those who are in need of us and to compromise in any differences that we may have, even in the case of other countries.

America is not perfect, but compared to the rest of the world, we are Utopia.

People in the past who wished to create Utopia dwelled on form the "whatness" of Utopia beginning with the questions about how to share, how to create an economy that is equitable, and how to include and construct sustainable practices that can be manageable and so forth.

These attempts, by some measure, did not prove to help to creating Utopian thinking; it is the people who has to be Utopian thinking. It is virtually impossible to have a Utopian society without Utopian-thinking people; this kind of thinking is needed in order to create a society for the "highest good for all." It is imperative that the society citizens have a conscious awareness of the highest god for all, and a Utopian society and its citizens has to be commensurate on the consciousness of the highest good for all. They go hand in hand to create this society model; when the people recognize this model, they will be inclined to replicate and move toward dedication to working toward creating this loving society. When this model is seen by the people, they will display feelings of a much happier society and will be apt to create more models, paradigms.

SUMMARY AND CLOSING THOUGHTS

> In order to change an existing paradigm, you do
> not struggle to try and change the problematic
> model. You create a new model and make
> the old one obsolete. That in essence is the
> higher service to which we are all called.
> —Buckminister Fuller

The garden of Eden is aligned and was accepted as an example for an originating Utopian work (Genesis 2).

Genesis' garden of Eden was considered Utopian before the modern Utopian thought. The garden portrayed a society existing free from evil, pain, illness, and want. In the garden of Eden, the inhabitants had only to adhere to the law of God which can be generalized as adherence to morality and hard work to keep the garden in sterile condition.

These thoughts of keeping within a "moral code" and working hard are alien thoughts but in a work of Utopia. The role of morality plays a reasonable role and is consistent to Utopian societies and is universal; it's founded on our ability to make the *right choices* and the acceptance that justice is the excellence and injustice as the "defect of the soul." The *Republic* and also a common part of Utopia relates to citizens who they are expecting to provide for the ones producing products that they require.

As in the garden of Eden, in Utopia, each individual is expected to give of themselves as much as they possibly can to the society, enough to be able to distribute to all members.

The exile of the inhabitants from the garden depicts the corruption that has removed "humanity from the Golden Age of the Original period of human felicity [the] idyllic state of ease, harmony, peace and plenty" (Murfin and Ray 205).

Humanity having been taught in perfection of the past and that moral development and tolerance are communitarianism provide for us a future that is better and continues in the search for the restoration of the "lost age." It is within literature and philosophy that has served as an instrument by which humanity can possibly be explored.

It is interesting how the concept Utopia began with being defined as a Greek word which means "no place" or at times "imaginary, not achievable." Today, it is a place, a society, a reality with major concerns about equality for all.

Utopia was defined at one time as a system of social perfection, and also, a Utopian Society was a group of people living together harmoniously; many more ideas have been cited as what a Utopian Society is like. Many were creative in their thinking and comprehensive taking into consideration the environment and economics as it relates to its citizens affording what they need and moving into other areas—technological, religious, and of course, political; politics play a major role in the governance of society which all is geared toward humanity. However, in my opinion, Utopia is in the middle of the spectrum—one being people caring for people and the politics in working together a Utopian Society.

THE UTOPIA IMPULSE

Plato's unseen realm is the place of ideas
in which are born and that humans
have access to, and therefore should
strive to access as much as possible.
                              —King James Bible

We, as people on this planet, have been reminded of *humankind* and the goal of humanity and our conscious awareness of the "highest good for all" and that we can achieve more happiness when we show love and respect for all people. It seems for the most part we have not listened because of our selfish desires. We tend to overlook the real and sincere essence of life and where true happiness lies.

There have been great speeches and songs said and written about America and how we can attain greatness and move forward to reach that goal.

Beginning with Plato's *Republic,* John Winthrop's speech, The Shining City Upon a Hill, Lyndon Johnson quoting from "America the Beautiful," and John F. Kennedy, in his death, commands what his life convey encouraging America to move forward. The time has come for Americans of all races and creeds and political beliefs to understand and to respect one another. And the beautiful lyrics of the song "America the Beautiful,"

God done shed his grace on thee; He crowned
thy good, yes hed did, in brotherhood.

To think Utopian is to respect and acknowledge the urgency of love for one another and the country; when this happens, we will have happiness at the ultimate.

Utopian thinking is not selfish nor it is color blind; Utopian thinking is togetherness.

Maybe we will not have a perfect society, but who knows, it is all in man's thinking.

I think that it would be a mistake for Americans to limit their thinking to the here and now, the truth about what the world could be, the truth is as what they see, but does what they see as truth renders them incapable to explore other worlds? Or what could they accept? Is it to think the world is already perfect?

Historically, America has had a fault line in that the races (Blacks and Whites) have had different versions of what they view of America as America promises hopes, ideologies, progress, and successes and despair.

Until the races come together in concert, see eye to eye, and collaboratively discuss these major differences, the hope for a perfect or a better society is nonexistent; Americans need to rid themselves of selfish desires, nonacceptance of those who are different in nationality, race, creed, and acknowledge and respect their contributions to the society as worthwhile and embrace it. There cannot be a perfect world. Perfect is faultless.

I believe in Henry Kissinger's words: "For other nations, Utopia is a blessed past, never to be recovered; For America, it is just beyond the horizon."

I feel compelled to argue the world for a better world; as a ninety-two-year-old woman, I sit in my old brown recliner in between rocks as new thoughts come forth.

BIBLIOGRAPHY

America as Utopia. reason.com/1987/03/01/america-as-utopia/.

America the Utopia Essay. The American Utopian. The United... cause hero.com ENGL.

American Imperialism. Boundless US History. courseslumenlearning. com/american-imperialism/.

Aristotelian. How to achieve a Utopia in a short amount of Time. Aristotelian part I and part 2.

Aristotelian. Social Order Part I, Part II.

Bodybuilding.com. misc. Socialism is Inevitable.

Card, Jean. America the Dystopia? Opinion contributor. May 13, 2016, 11:45 A.M.

Chaganti, Anka. Does America "Truly Have Equality in Its Practices?" St. John Creek, Georgia, November 28, 2016.

Chasing Utopia: A Photographer Uncovers Visionary New Deal-Era Towns. Nation Trust for Historic Preservation. 8:00 a.m., October 13, 2018.

College Term Paper. Is America Becoming a Godless Culture? www. collegetermpapers/Religion/is-A.

Crèvecœur, Hector, J. The New Man. November 6, 2013.

Davis, Victor Hanson. Disenchantment American—Politics and Policy. opinion January 7, 2005.

Durant, Will. *The Pleasures of Philosophy*. p. 279. Others see education as a threat to God and state, and there would be no need for either of them.

E.H. Carr. A Critique of Utopianism: The Necessity of Utopian Thinking—Cross-National Citizens. Booth, 1991; Boyle 2004; Kamp, 2008; Brincat 2009.

Explore the Garden of Eden Bible. Thought Co. Garden of Eden.

Fallows, James. *How America Can Rise Again. The* Atlantic. January/ February 2010 issue.

Forbes Media LLC.

Garden of Eden, From Utopia to Dystopia. Prezi, prezi.com/bmzued _8/garden of Eden.

Gopnik, Adam. Four Nineteenth Authors Office. Blueprints for a better world. July 23, 2018.

Hankinson, BP. In Pursuit of Happiness. February 19, 2013.

How Utopia Shaped the World. www.bbc.com/culture/article/20160920-how-utopia-shaped-the-world.

Insiders View. *Is it Utopia Yet?: An Insiders View of Twin Oaks Community.* 1994.

John Winthrop Dreams of a City on a Hill, 1630 www.Mt.holy.edu. acad/intel/winthrop.htm.

Kapur, Akash. *Th_e Return of the Utopians. The New Yorker.*

Kelly, Jack. *Dystopian Nation? Not Quite: Here's Where America Is Doing Well. Forbes.* August 9, 2019, 11:00 a.m.

Kerwick, Jack. *America-as-Idea: A Fiction with Many Uses.* March 15, 2018.

King, Branden. *Is America Dead, Deferred or Just Different.* American University of Cincinnati.

Le Guin, Ursula K. *The Ones Who Walked Away from Omelas.* 1973 Philosophical fiction.

Mganboi, Nyeusi Nguvu. "Black Utopia: Nation. Black Power." June 26, 2012. Ranger Utopia Nation Building 88, Filed in Society of Black Power Ranger Utopia.

Nesbit, Robert. *America as Utopia.* Reason.com. March, 1981 issue.

Newberg, Michael. "The American Ethos of Patriotism and Melting into a New race of Men Whose Labor and Prosperity Will One Day Cause Great Changes in the World." 607.

Newman, Sandra. "The Other Side of the Black Mirror: Literary Utopias Offer the Seeds of Better Real Life." The Guardian. com.

Paul Hollander and the Anatomy of Discontent. October 8, 2014/B/S/ Archive.

Packer, George. *Summary and Analysis of the Unwinding: An Inner History of the New America.*

Red Letter Christians. *Christian Utopia and the Body Politic.*

Robertson, Michael. *The Last Utopians: Four Late 19th Century Visionaries and their Legacy.*

Rogers, James. *The Meaning of the "Pursuit of Happiness."* firstthings. com/web-exclusives/2012/06/the-meaning-of-the-pursuit-of-happiness.

Schreiter, Kobert J. "Roads to Reconciliation." Catholic Theolyn.

Shavings, Brian. "An American Experiment with Socialism." brian-shavings.com/2008/10/. An early American experiment. 2008.

Smithsonian. The Neverending Hunt for Utopia. History. John's vision.

Stoner, Evan. An inclusive America America. Medium.com/@even-stoner/9/. An inclusive America.

Summary and Analysis Boo II: The Discourse on Utopia: Learning.

Sunday Dialogue: A Disillusioned Citizenry. https://www.nytimes. com/2013/10/06/opinion/sunday/sunday-dialogue-a-disillu-sioned-citizenry.html. Oct. 5, 2013.

The American Dream. "Theft by Deception: The Immigration on Game. How Politicians Are Robbing Citizens Access to the American Dream." Wed. June 17, 2015.

The Blaze. *Is-There-Hope-for-America-Shedding-some-Light-On-A-Darkening-World.* www.the Atlantic.com/contributions/is-there-hope.

The Garden of Eden. Genesis 1:26–31. Brit Library. www.bl.ok/ utopia/perfection/genesis/genesis12613.

Theologies of American exceptualism: Winthrop and Cavell. https://tif. ssrc.org/2017/02/13/winthrop-and-cavell/

Utopia Makes a Comeback. We Live in a Political World. www.gapat-ton.net/2016/10/297-utopia-makes-comeback.

Webb, Danen. Talk. "Off the Shelf, Literary Festival: The Need for Utopian Now Parts of Sheffield." Oct 24, 2017.

Wikipedia. *The Giver.* America. https://en.wikipedia.org/wiki/ The_Giver.

Word Power Reconciliation Healing Past Building the Future.

ABOUT THE AUTHOR

Blanche Parker is the youngest of six siblings and was born in St. Augustine, Florida. Her parents died; while an infant, she was reared by an aunt who dedicated herself to seeing that they were educated and that they trust in God. A love for learning was not always the best, but she always tried her best.

She attended a small Liberal Arts Christian College and studied political and social sciences on the secondary level. Later on, she studied science and humanities and earned BS and master's degrees in science and humanities and postgraduate on doctorate.

She taught and trained workers in a head start setting and taught elementary school. She then received the teacher of the year award in her school, the governor teacher's award, and many acknowledges of appreciation award. Her first teaching assignment was in 1947 in a one-room schoolhouse.

CPSIA information can be obtained
at www.ICGtesting.com
Printed in the USA
LVHW112339140921
697829LV00001B/154